Painted Paragraphs

BOOKS BY DONALD NEWLOVE

Novels

The Painter Gabriel

Sweet Adversity
embodying the author's final
revisions of his Siamese twin novels,
Leo & Theodore and *The Drunks*

Eternal Life

Curranne Trueheart

Starlite Photoplays
a trilogy embodying the completed and forthcoming

Marlon and Meryl Together at Last:
A Village Romance

Buckangel:
A Screwball Tragedy Starring Cary Grant

The Welles Requiem

On Writing

Those Drinking Days:
Myself and Other Writers

First Paragraphs:
Inspired Openings for Writers and Readers

Painted Paragraphs:
Inspired Description for Writers and Readers

Invented Voices:
Inspired Dialogue for Writers and Readers

A HANDBOOK FOR THE SOUL

Painted Paragraphs

INSPIRED DESCRIPTION FOR WRITERS AND READERS

DONALD NEWLOVE

HENRY HOLT AND COMPANY NEW YORK

Henry Holt and Company, Inc.
Publishers since 1866
115 West 18th Street
New York, New York 10011

Henry Holt® is a registered trademark
of Henry Holt and Company, Inc.

Published in Canada by Fitzhenry & Whiteside Ltd.,
195 Allstate Parkway, Markham, Ontario L3R 4T8.

Library of Congress Cataloging-in-Publication Data
Newlove, Donald.
Painted paragraphs: inspired description for writers
and readers: a handbook for the soul/Donald Newlove.—1st ed.
          p.   cm.
          Includes index.
      I. Title. II. Title: Handbook for the soul.
PN218.N49   1993   93-22168
808'.02—dc20   CIP

ISBN 0-8050-2978-8
ISBN 0-8050-2591-X (An Owl Book: pbk.)

Henry Holt books are available for special promotions
and premiums. For details contact: Director, Special Markets.

First published in hardcover in 1993 by
Henry Holt and Company, Inc.

First Owl Book Edition—1995

DESIGNED BY PAULA R. SZAFRANSKI

Printed in the United States of America
All first editions are printed on acid-free paper.∞

1   3   5   7   9   10   8   6   4   2
1   3   5   7   9   10   8   6   4   2
                (pbk.)

A Letter to the Reader

Great description shakes us. It fills our lungs with the life of its author. Suddenly he sings within us. Someone else has seen life as we see it! And the voice that fills us, should the writer be dead, bridges the gulf between life and death. Great description is stronger than death.

Painted Paragraphs: Inspired Description for Writers and Readers follows *First Paragraphs: Inspired Openings for Writers and Readers,* my first handbook. That shows writers gathering their powers for a godlike first paragraph written on Olympus. It is about the white-hot opening whose glow speaks for a story's greatest strength: its spirit.

Painted Paragraphs is about description that breathes out of the writer's breast. Call it landscape with soul. But it's about more than physical landscape; it's more truly about spiritual landscape, the weathers within, and I gather herein some gorgeous pages. That gorgeousness, however, shimmers from the writer's spirit. A writer is his landscape. Feeling is all, mere rendering of things not much. The picturesque is for Sunday painters.

Please don't think my thoughts in this book make up a style guide. The only rules I measure by are inspiration and making sense—or enough sense to sink me body and soul into the writing. If you think Proust's paragraphs herein, or Hemingway's fishing or Whitman's poems, follow rules, you're blinkered. You've been diddled by the critics. Yes, Whitman builds on a scheme that lends emotional underlining—but it's not a scheme handed down to him by the lords of rhetoric and prosody. His rules come from his breast and are shaped by his breath.

Writing in the West usually follows a movement toward climax: landscape and splendid decoration are not enough. Whitman's poems work toward a moment of emotional enlargement, not toward the usual "turn" at the end in which a poem's meaning grows by reversing itself or capping what has gone before. Hemingway's "Big Two-Hearted River" works toward an understanding by his hero, Nick, that the darkness of the swamp he dare not enter mirrors the darkness he carries within him from the war in Italy. But even here Hemingway arrived at his big spark at the last moment, deciding before publication to chop off the story's last nine pages and stop with Nick's thoughts about the swamp. He threw out the rubbish, and with trimmed pages had a larger, stronger story. In "Los Angeles

Notebook" Joan Didion devises her story backward, by going from its passage of greatest tension to a spiritual flatness that leaves her splayed lifeless, and achieves a form that resembles the spirit-killing effects of Los Angeles weather during the Santa Ana season of "bad winds." From Proust to Didion the method is to let an ignited spine tell the story. This is not to say writers don't have tongue-loosening tricks, or make sly power shifts in a story's energies, or woo belief with disarming hocus-pocus. A pinch of artful cheating is much like making use of God-given accidents and typos. Just don't get caught at it. But even bagging another man's thought is okay if you do more with it than he did. Whitman's "To the Man-of-War-Bird" embezzles by paraphrase an English translation of a passage in French about the great seabird and from this theft shapes a peerless poem. Few remember the plundered original.

The last book in my trilogy, which is also available, is *Invented Voices: Inspired Dialogue for Writers and Readers.* Once again, this is not about craft but about the writer's breath. A writer is all his characters, and must be, if they are to speak with strength about themselves and their acts. Every devil is a prince in the writer's heart, which is a confessional given over to murderers and adulterers. Goethe loves Mephistopheles, thinks he's a well-spoken, colorful devil, and the author of the Book of Job loves Satan, a fallen angel still on speaking terms with God, and Milton gives his best lines to the snake. No man, or devil, disgusts the writer. Our job in part is to find within us just how the devil split off from our better natures. Iago is Othello's worst, most hidden face, one that Othello can't bear to look at in himself, and in Iago Shakespeare's pity is infinite. Once the writer sets out to scalp a character, he scalps his own soul. We must kiss the assassin and hug him to us. Let him speak from a wholeness of heart. Iago has his soliloquies.

Let me mention *Those Drinking Days: Myself and Other Writers,* my autobiography, which tells about my days as Drunkspeare the Inspired. That book shows how alcohol stunned many geniuses and why many great American writers would have left a larger shelf of first-rate works, with fewer duds, had they abandoned the bottle. *Those Drinking Days* sounds the first notes of the themes in my present trilogy for writers and readers.

—D.N.

Painted Paragraphs

One starry night I walked home from the movies, an agony gnawing at me.

Twenty and just freed from the Marines after World War II, I carried at my side Thomas Wolfe's heavy, endless *Of Time and the River.* My family lived on elm-lined Lakeview Avenue in my small New York hometown of Jamestown. I'd just seen *The Blue Dahlia,* a listless, unbelievable murder mystery with Alan Ladd. Poor though I thought the film, its theme of veterans returning to their native streets pierced me. A kind of postwar blues or chewing on the hearts of young servicemen suddenly back home had been cast onto the screen. I longed to write about the real feelings at work in me, untouched by Hollywood glamour or Ladd's pompadour and Veronica Lake's falsely perfect peekaboo wave.

Could I put these starry deeps and lamplighted elms into words that sang like the nightwind now rinsing my senses and shivering the spring leaves?

My yearnings about *The Blue Dahlia* were not simply to re-create my own postwar mood by working up the signs of the times, the songs and cigarette packages, the bleakness or promise of the streets and stores, the look of houses and the postwar light on people's faces. Painting these things, or a rock, a door, or an alley that is not as lived in as Van Gogh's painting of his beaten-up shoes (which could be Christ's were Christ alive in Holland), is not personal—they could be painted by any writer with a gift for realism. But when Hemingway tells us:

> A girl came into the cafe and sat by herself at a table near the window. She was very pretty with a face fresh as a newly minted coin if they minted coins in smooth flesh with rain-freshened skin, and her hair was black as a crow's wing and cut sharply and diagonally across her cheek.
>
> —*A Moveable Feast* (1964)

and, on the next page,

> As I ate the oysters with their strong taste of the sea and their faint metallic taste that the cold white wine washed away, leaving only the sea taste and the succulent texture, and as I drank their cold liquid from each shell and washed it down with the crisp taste of the wine, I lost the empty feeling and began to be happy and to make plans.

we enjoy a gift not merely for words and stuff learned from books, but much more: a style inspired by a man's grip on life. In the rhythms of the lean, long sentences we feel the whole man breathing. Hemingway wrote about that girl's black crow's wing and those sea-tasting oysters and that white wine that took away his empty feeling and made him happy and full of plans *forty years* after he experienced them! At first we fear that newly-minted-coin cliché, until he smiles lightly and frames her new-minted shine with the unforgettable black crow's wing cutting sharply and diagonally across her cheek of smooth flesh and rain-freshened skin. (Don't ignore his smile, which sets us up to accept the full sensuality of her skin.) Then the food passage, which might easily fall into banality, turns out to be not simply about the sensations of eating, marvelously rendered though they are, but about a change in spirit in which the food is only the taxi which takes him from an empty feeling to upwelling happiness and a bloom of plans. Surely these two passages set the morning stars singing for Hemingway, who rose daily at dawn and wrote with his senses at their coolest and freshest under the real morning stars. "As soon after first light as possible," he said.

We also sense moral force, and that Hemingway gives us absolutely the way things were, in words untainted by any thought other than to enrich us. The life in these passages arises from our delight in his ice-clear freshness of vision, which has focused on a grain of sand and secreted around it a pearl that has been gathering painfully in his spirit for forty years. This ball of luster must be spoken, given away with a piece of his heart, and lodged where it will never be lost to memory: in other people. He will never own that pearl until he gives it away and ensures its immortal life. The moral genius gives his heart away, not his skill with words, though his phrases be heady as crushed mint. Any ad writer can crush mint or paint a rose.

Here is how God writes description, using the nameless storyteller who wrote the Book of Job:

> Why are you using your ignorance to deny my providence? Now get ready to fight, for I am going to demand some answers from you, and you must reply.
>
> Where were you when I laid the foundations of the earth? Tell me, if you know so much. Do you know how its dimensions were determined, and who did the surveying? What supports its foundations, and who laid its cornerstone, as the morning stars sang together and all the angels shouted for joy?
>
> Who decreed the boundaries of the seas when they gushed from the womb? Who clothed them with clouds and thick darkness, and barred them by limiting their shores, and said, "Thus far and no farther shall you come, and here shall your proud waves stop!"
>
> —Job 38:1–11

Why is God so high-and-mighty with Job, such a Big Mouth? He's in pain! He's got to lay it out for Job, verse by verse, show him just how he commanded the morning to appear and caused the dawn to rise in the east, then picked up the corners of the night and shook the wicked out of it.

"Have you explored the springs from which the seas come, or walked in the sources of their depths?" he asks Job. "Has the location of the gates of Death been revealed to you? Do you realize the extent of the earth? Tell me about it if you know!"

Job doesn't know, though if he were a poet he'd not fail for answers. The Hebrew poet who wrote the Book of Job trades in part on his people's eagerness to know the mystic heart of landscape. A few verses later the poet/God asks Job, "Who dug the gullies for the torrents of rain, or made a path for the thunderbolts?" He shoves Job's eyes down into his homeland's gullies, excites him with torrents of rain, all familiar stuff, then zings him with making "a path for the thunderbolts," raising Job's mind to the mystical, and then hits him with some Big Bolts:

> Can you hold back the stars? Can you restrain Orion or Pleiades? Can you ensure the proper sequence of the seasons, or guide the constellation of the Bear with her satellites across the heavens? Do you know the laws of the universe and how the heavens influence the earth? Can you shout to the clouds and make it rain? Can you make lightning appear and cause it to strike as you direct it?

> —Job 38:31–35

Why does the Hebrew poet put himself into God's shoes and bloody Job with all this? Because he's mysticizing him as a member of the tribe and making sure that no common disaster will part Job from the faith. He shrinks Job to an atom, a thing weak and willful when no God fills his mind. Only the imagination of this poet and his genius for moral landscape can awaken Job at depths never before known by the sufferer. And at last Job says, "Now mine eye seeth thee," and he is moved to self-loathing and repentance in dust and ashes.

Tribal life under huge bending skies, be it Sioux or Hebrew tribe, may empower description with great spiritual force. Here John Edgar Wideman tells us of a tree out front of his mother's house in Homewood, the black section of Pittsburgh:

A massive tree centuries old holds out against the odds here across from my mother's house, one of the biggest trees in Pittsburgh, anchored in a green tangle of weeds and bushes, trunk thick as a Buick, black as night after rain soaks its striated hide. Huge spread of its branches canopies the foot of the hill where the streets come together. Certain times of day in summer it shades my mother's front porch. If it ever tore loose from its moorings, it would crush her house like a sledgehammer. As big as it is, its roots must run under her cellar. The sound of it drinking, lapping nourishment deep underground is part of the quiet when her house is empty. How the tree survived a city growing around it is a mystery. For years no more than a twig, a sapling, a switch someone could have snapped off to beat a balky animal, swat a child's behind. I see a dark fist exploding through the asphalt, thrusting to the sky, the fingers opening, multiplying, fanning outward to form a vast umbrella of foliage. The arm behind it petrifies, other thick limbs burst from knots of hardened flesh, each one duplicating the fan of leaves, the delicate network of branches, thinning, twisting as they climb higher and farther from the source. Full-blown in a matter of seconds, ready to stand there across from my mother's house forever, till its time to be undone in the twinkling of an eye, just the way it arrived.

—"All Stories Are True" (1991),
The Stories of John Edgar Wideman

Later in this story a second tree is described, in a prison yard, which Wideman's brother hopes someday to climb, when it's high enough, to escape over the forty-foot wall. Both trees might be called tribal trees. They tell us thrillingly about the first encounter of blacks with Pittsburgh, the mystery of a sapling that becomes a dark fist exploding upward, fingers multiplying, fanning outward, the trunk turning to stone as other thick limbs burst from its hardened knots of "flesh" still fanning outward, while the roots go running and drinking under the cellar—the house empty, they can even be heard lapping. All the detail in this description, from the tree being anchored in a green tangle of weeds and bushes, where the streets come together, to the solemn humor of the trunk being thick as a Buick (a big gas-eater once favored by blacks as being just next to a Cadillac), has a folk echo that makes the tree ("black as night after rain soaks its striated hide") a vivid picture of black life in Iron City, as Pittsburgh is called. The tree in the prison yard is a frail thing to pin one's hope on, but Wideman's brother has turned himself into the tree back home, through body-building:

My brother's arms are prison arms. The kind you see in the street that clue you where a young brother's been spending his time. Bulging biceps, the rippled look of ropy sinews

7

and cords of muscle snaking around the bones. Skinned. Excess flesh boiled away in this cauldron. Must be noisy as a construction site where the weightlifters hang out in the prison yard. Metal clanking. Grunts and groans. Iron pumped till shoulders and chests swell to the bursting point. Men fashioning arms thick enough to wrestle fate, hold off the pressure of walls and bars always bearing down. Large. Big. Nothing else to do all day. Size one measure of time served. Serious time. Bodies honed to stop-time perfection, beyond vulnerability and pain. I see them in their sun-scoured playground sprawled like dazed children.

The largeness of Wideman's power—the "thick limbs burst from knots of hardened flesh" in the trees are the bodybuilders' bulging biceps and "the rippled look of ropy sinews and cords of muscle snaking around the bones"—emerges in part from his muting these likenesses between the prisoners and the great tree of black life in Pittsburgh. He lets the tree's thick limbs and the men's bulging biceps come together in our unconscious with a sense of bitter song rising from the heart of his people. He is as much the poet bonding his people into a common faith as is the Hebrew poet of Job—and in Wideman's stories Job's disasters are no worse than those known to blacks. Remember, though, that the power comes from exactly seen facts, which then glow and take force from moral purpose. A less purposeful writer, drugged by words, might have carried the bodybuilding too far and pushed too hard on the tree for the jangle of anguish, but Wideman brings off his inner meaning with no strain or sense of twisting iron pokers into muscle-bound knots of argument. Each picture comes from what John Donne calls a naked thinking heart.

Walt Whitman, too, gains energy from moral purpose in description so original that he was damned for writing it, although he is as strong in scope as the poet of Job. All of "I Sing the Body Electric" is a highwatermark of outspokenness in the English tongue. In the ninth and last section Whitman makes a statement that would leave the nineteenth century flabbergasted:

> O my body! I dare not desert the likes of you in other men
>   and women, nor the likes of the parts of you,
> I believe the likes of you are to stand or fall with the
>   likes of the soul, (and that they are the soul,)
> I believe the likes of you shall stand or fall with my poem,
>   and that they are my poems,
> Man's, woman's, child's, youth's, wife's, husband's,
>   mother's, father's, young man's, young woman's
>   poems,
> Head, neck, hair, ears, drop and tympan of the ears,
> Eyes, eye-fringes, iris of the eye, eyebrows, and the waking
>   or sleeping of the lids,
> Mouth, tongue, lips, teeth, roof of the mouth, jaws, and
>   the jaw-hinges,
> Nose, nostrils of the nose, and the partition,
> Cheeks, temples, forehead, chin, throat, back of the neck,
>   neck-slue,
> Strong shoulders, manly beard, scapula, hind-shoulders,
>   and the ample side-round of the chest,
> Upper-arm, armpit, elbow-socket, lower-arm,
>   arm-sinews, arm-bones,
> Wrist and wrist-joints, hand, palm, knuckles, thumb,
>   forefinger, finger-joints, finger-nails,

Broad breast-front, curling hair of the breast, breast-
bone, breast-side,
Ribs, belly, backbone, joints of the backbone,
Hips, hip-sockets, hip-strength, inward and outward
round, man-balls, man-root,
Strong set of thighs, well carrying the trunk above,
Leg-fibres, knee, knee-pan, upper-leg, under-leg,
Ankles, instep, foot-ball, toes, toe-joints, the heel;
All attitudes, all the shapeliness, all the belongings of my
or your body or of any one's body, male or female,
The lung-sponges, the stomach-sac, the bowels sweet and
clean,
The brain in its folds inside the skull-frame,
Sympathies, heart-valves, palate-valves, sexuality,
maternity,
Womanhood, and all that is a woman, and the man that
comes from woman,
The womb, the teats, nipples, breast-milk, tears, laughter,
weeping, love-looks, love-perturbations and risings,
The voice, articulation, language, whispering, shouting
aloud,
Food, drink, pulse, digestion, sweat, sleep, walking,
swimming,
Poise on the hips, leaping, reclining, embracing, arm-
curving and tightening,
The continual changes of the flex of the mouth, and
around the eyes,
The skin, the sunburnt shade, freckles, hair,
The curious sympathy one feels when feeling with the
hand the naked meat of the body,

The circling rivers the breath, and breathing it in and
  out,
The beauty of the waist, and thence of the hips, and
  thence downward toward the knees,
The thin red jellies within you or within me, the bones
  and the marrow in the bones,
The exquisite realization of health;
O I say these are not the parts and poems of the body only,
  but of the soul,
O I say now these are the soul!

—"I Sing the Body Electric" (1855),
Leaves of Grass, Walt Whitman

This fearless triumph stunned readers back in 1855 and is still a poem that would put any poet on the map, had he the wit to think of it. Its anatomical inventory at first looks quite dense but is really a light skim of the body's parts whose names set forth powerfully Whitman's great argument that the body is the soul and should not be surrendered to anyone any more than you'd surrender your soul, and further that these parts of himself are the likes of the soul in other human bodies. He thinks he heralds a new American folk poetry with frank verses like these. What ambition!

Whitman's awakening from dull everyday thought at thirty-five was a great miracle, one we know little about but which he described as God baring the poet's bosom-bone one transparent summer morning and licking his bare-stript heart. That's a good way to put it, when we think of the enlightened man who was born at that moment. There's no exact way for him to speak of this sea change, so he tells us "the words of my book nothing, the drift everything." Clearly, though, he carries a bag of charged details that ache in his testicles: "the life-lit eyes" (as earlier in the poem he calls them) are not only the eyes of a slave at auction but are as well the first early impression of the bulging life-lit eyes of mice, the faithful eyes of dogs, the patient eyes of his mother quietly placing the dishes on the supper table, the help-seeking eyes of his retarded brother, Eddie, for whom he cared all his life, and his own strange eyes, hooded, patient, clear as brookwater and as untouched by horror or love as a doll's eyes. Man to man Whitman did not give of his deepest being, but only of a comradely feeling. He did not engage you in argument. All that part of him lay reserved for verse, where the only fight was with himself, not with you. His character became one vast acceptance of what arose before him, but our angers and arguments are not his. Not that he was untouched, only that he was untouchable. This reserved quality allows an immense freshness to lines committed to paper. His word resolves no dispute, but falls on the page with original purity, like a boy's first sperm.

What I'm talking about is the sources of description. Each of us has a home within, first memories of town or countryside to which our heart turns for refreshment and plenty. My earliest template is of Erie, Pennsylvania, during the Depression. I see Erie in shades of gray. In fact, my sense of color never arose until I was in my teens, living in Jamestown, and the lushness of alcohol pricked my eyes awake. Then color overwhelmed me, and I saw that not just MGM musicals but reality itself drenched me with blues and gold and the deep blood of a maple leaf. Or perhaps . . . Jamestown itself, a town famed for its hills and red-brick streets and towering elms. The green air swam. I remember the God-given ache of my first spring in adolescence, walking home from school dizzy with grass-smells and first noticing that the girls ahead carrying their books against their chests had hips more low-slung than mine.

My mother and I had lived in downtown Erie during the thirties and at five I began running the largely treeless downtown streets amid fruit carts and manure and horseflies. When we moved to Jamestown in 1938, it was like coming ashore in the Bermudas. These two geographies set the tones of landscape which still urge for life in my writing. And as much as the hills of home in my adolescence lent my writer's heart a green songfulness, it's Erie that grips me with endless crowds on busy, drained granite. I dash through tall legs on my way to hot oily Virginia redskins at the Mr. Peanut shop or to empty lots I haunt by broken factory windows and I watch trash burn in big drums or sit at a trestle table in the blue tobacco fumes of a bingo parlor. The vanilla-heavy smell of candy corn in Woolworth's floods me, I hear the sizzle of spark-dripping trolley cars, race to the faded red-brick pile of my grade school and find the playground gravel empty on Saturday morning, hurtle down now longlost garage-filled alleys winding midblock, stumble into the amazing matchbox darkness of my first moviehouse, pound up the stairway to our second-floor apartment into our cramped living room and boxy bedroom, and on a winter morning find icy thumbs of cream pushing up paper bottle caps in our steel milkbox. Wide streets hold dense dark firs and tree-sheltered houses with stepped lawns rising to high porches and like a dog with no sense of property I run between any houses into any backyard, where I find a sunstruck garden full of big bending hollyhocks. Side streets and atomized alleys where I ran can mist my eyes even today, not sentimentally but with animal loss—I left a child's legs there and have been searching for them ever since. I see myself at five or six in stony lots or running full tilt to the Saturday serials or walking wide-eyed down a street never before taken but strange with back-yard fences, weeds, asphalt, old tires and charged with a moiling dark shadow that makes my heart pump with desire to sneak into hidden places, through basement windows, or into a store closed on Sunday whose back window is unlocked. I have compassion for that dog of a boy chewing on lumps of hot tar from the newly laid midsummer street, his small palms and bare legs streaked with black. Compassion for him gives the same moral force to memory I find in love for any child I know today. All children are impacted into a landscape of loss.

I was born into a mother's love and then allowed to swim for myself, becoming at five, and six, and seven a Marco Polo of the great city of Erie, searching it out from our three rooms over the Mayflower Bar and racing far afield to the Nickel Plate trainyards and down to the rust-colored freighters at the city docks with their floating rats and orange peel and out to the city sewer drains where without knowing it I waded in a brown swamp of shit.

Hers was the face of love and I see her now at the great round blue mirror of her vanity, tracing lines on her plucked brows and deepening the starlight of her youth, my movie beauty who worked in clubs and brought home well-heeled boyfriends for love scenes on the couch. I lived with a goddess. Hers was the face of my conscience, or something deeper than the face, she was the ground within where I battled myself daily and lost and hid behind lies on a straight face she saw through like glass.

So what do I mean by moral force, and by moral force in description?

The great lift we feel in the description in Job is that of God the Father awakening a sinless earth within us. His great slap makes us breathe and cry at once at the foundations of the sea within us and at the first burning invasion of lake and cloud or sight of the big red ball of sunset or first sense of the bending immensity of the earth or awe of the limitless charged depths of the night sky. Or in my case, God the Mother, turning my eyes into her ("Look at me, my son"), *She* who has laid out gullies for her torrents of love, and created me to mirror the seal of character on her lips, and then set me free on the streets of Erie where I burn with crime and rocket down alleys and over stony lots and must be home at five-thirty. Beans and franks, Flash Gordon, bed.

Here is how two other writers remember earlier days, one by way of food, the other by a medicine chest:

When she opened the cupboards, an ache slid down her forehead into her nasal passage and throbbed on the roof of each nostril. It continued like an arrow into her skull, and skated up and down her neck until it had no place else to go. Mildred gave her head a good shake. Bags of black-eyed peas, pinto beans, butter beans, lima beans, and a big bag of rice stared her in the face. She opened another cabinet and there sat half a jar of peanut butter, a can of sweet peas and carrots, one can of creamed corn, and two cans of pork-n-beans. There was nothing in the refrigerator except a few crinkly apples she'd gotten from the apple man two weeks ago, a stick of margarine, four eggs, a quart of milk, a box of lard, a can of Pet milk, and a two-inch piece of salt pork.

She put on a pot of pinto beans. Mildred knew the kids

were tired of them, and so was she, but at least they would last a few days. . . . She chopped up a yellow onion and sat it on the table, then took the lonely piece of salt pork from the refrigerator. She threw them both into the pot, sneezed, then wiped her tearing eyes. The only time Mildred cried on her own accord was when she peeled onions.

. . . By six o'clock, the beans were thick and simmered but the house had grown colder and colder. . . . Mildred made [the children] huddle in front of the warm open oven while they ate their beans and rice and corn bread. She wasn't hungry and just sipped her last beer.

—*Mama* (1987), Terry McMillan

Mildred is Mama Peacock, twenty-seven, who single-handedly raises her five children in the black ghetto of Point Haven, Michigan. Her story covers more than twenty years, during which this spirited, resourceful woman works as a cleaning woman, a nursing home helper, on an assembly line, and briefly takes up whoring. In the passage above, the furnace has broken down and the cupboard gives her a headache. Aside from Pet milk, nothing has a brand name and all detail is general and weighted with sadness. McMillan might have brought in the shelves and cans more finely, bound us with mouse droppings on the shelf paper, the supermarket labels, the cow on the Pet milk, but chose instead simply to splash everything down and point out the weary varieties of the beans, the wrinkled apples, the lonely lump of salt pork. Great darkness floods from the thud of simple words, the limas, the navy, pinto, butter beans, sweet peas, carrots, rice, two cans of pork-n-beans, the box of lard.

Did McMillan have to research this description, work it up? Not a bit. It clearly floated out of her chest onto the page, although these cans may have weighed down her shoulders as she wrote the passage. And that's the delight of it, shedding the inner landscape of one's childhood and giving it to others. As it happens, Mildred's eldest daughter, Freda, gets a college degree and becomes a writer. Those cans of beans are medals from her daughter. See, Mama, I didn't forget.

Set that description beside this one by Jerome Salinger. We watch Mrs. Bessie Glass, the mother of seven fiercely bright, once-famous children, go through her medicine chest while her now twenty-five-year-old son Zooey takes a bath behind a nylon shower curtain:

She opened its mirror-faced door and surveyed the congested shelves with the eye—or, rather, the masterly squint—of a dedicated medicine-cabinet gardener. Before her, in overly luxuriant rows, was a host, so to speak, of golden pharmaceuticals, plus a few technically less indigenous whatnots. The shelves bore iodine, Mercurochrome, vitamin capsules, dental floss, aspirin, Anacin, Bufferin, Argyrol, Musterole, Ex-Lax, Milk of Magnesia, Sal Hepatica, Aspergum, two Gillette razors, one Schick Injector razor, two tubes of shaving cream, a bent and somewhat torn snapshot of a fat black-and-white cat asleep on a porch railing, three combs, two hairbrushes, a bottle of Fitch Dandruff Remover, a small, unlabelled box of glycerine suppositories, Vicks Nose Drops, Vicks VapoRub, six bars of castile soap, the stubs of three tickets to a 1946 musical comedy ("Call Me Mister"), a tube of depilatory cream, a box of Kleenex, two seashells, an assortment of used-looking emery boards, two jars of cleansing cream, three pairs of scissors, a nail file, an unclouded blue marble (known to marble shooters, at least in the twenties, as a "purey"), a cream for contracting enlarged pores, a pair of tweezers, the strapless chassis of a girl's or woman's gold wristwatch, a box of bicarbonate of soda, a girl's boarding-school class ring with a chipped onyx stone, a bottle of Stop-ette—and, inconceivably or no, quite a good deal more. . . . She nudged an unopened box of Sal Hepatica a little with the trowel of her extended fingers to align it with the other sempervirents in its row, and then closed the cabinet door. . . .

—*Franny and Zooey* (1961), J. D. Salinger

This inventory, which I once thought daring, and still admire, bears a kind of cuckoo poetry in its gathering of "golden pharmaceuticals." ("Sempervirents" keep you "always fresh.") But what kind of feeling do you get from it? Well, mine is that it's worked up. It's a great stunt, but no weight that Salinger has to lift off his heart nor even something joyously haywire he wants to amuse us with. "Zooey" in *Franny and Zooey* is more high-flown than funny. It's told in a lofty, worldly-wise voice that moves along by slow mouthfuls of words, with many asides to swallow, and is bookish and stylized as a Venetian screen. Today it reads slaved over. Now I may be wrong, and Salinger had a gay old time writing it. But my brain gets soggy watching him bend phrases into a likeness of the human voice.

When Thomas Wolfe sneaks into a millionaire's kitchen for a midnight snack and tells us of what he finds there, we know that his words are rooted in a greedy child who raises food into fantasy: it is such a kitchen as he has never seen before.

Crammed with every staple and cook's necessity, stocked with dainties from all the earth's weathers and markets, canned corn, bottled fruits and crocks of cheese, all the olive and pickle relishes as well as anchovies, herrings and sardines. Here are boxes of crystallized fruits, spicy Chinese ginger in wicker jars, rich jellies "green as emerald, red as rubies, smoother than whipped cream," here are vinegars and virgin oils. Everything you can think of!

Food! Food, indeed! . . . Even as the eye glistened and the mouth began to water at the sight of a noble roast of beef, all crisp and crackly in its cold brown succulence, the attention was diverted to a plump broiled chicken, whose brown and crackly tenderness fairly seemed to beg for the sweet and savage pillage of the tooth. But now a pungent and exciting fragrance would assail the nostrils: it was the smoked pink slices of an Austrian ham—should it be brawny bully beef, now, or the juicy breast of a white tender pullet, or should it be the smoky pungency, the half-nostalgic savor of the Austrian ham? . . .

What shall it be now? What shall it be? A snack! A snack!—before we prowl the meadows of the moon tonight, and soak our hearts in the moonlight's magic and the visions of our youth—what shall it be before we prowl the meadows of the moon? Oh, it shall be a snack, a snack—hah! hah! . . . a slice or two of that pink Austrian ham that smells so sweet and pungent . . . I'll have a slice of this roast beef, as well . . . a slice of red rare meat there at the centre—ah-h! . . . a slice of that plump chicken—some white meat, thank you, at the breast—ah, there it is!—how sweetly doth the noble fowl submit to the swift and keen persuasion of the knife—

and now, perhaps . . . a spoonful of those lima beans, as gay
as April and as sweet as butter . . . a snack—a snack—

—*Of Time and the River* (1935), Thomas Wolfe

You can tell that smoked Austrian ham has him hooked.
This rhapsody (here *much* abridged) is a set piece, the kind of
aside that I look forward to most eagerly in Wolfe, knowing
that his moments when he's as unbuttoned as Beethoven come
from an ecstasy denied most writers as they stick to their story
lines. It's an inventory much like dozens of those in Whitman
(recall his anatomical inventory in "I Sing the Body Electric").
In its self-mockery it's more together than many of Wolfe's
rhapsodies, which tend to go on and on like Richard Strauss
writing "The Alpine Symphony" and not finding a shape for
what he's saying.

A note of high seriousness comes in earlier when Wolfe suggests a big theme behind his rhapsody—The American Icebox
at Midnight—as if he's striving for an inventory in the same
league as Whitman's in "The Sleepers," another night piece.
Does the theme of gluttony deliver something from Wolfe's
deepest heart, which he can speak of only in mockery? Well, he
has another set piece about food (among many) which strikes a
more serious chord and is closer to Whitman in voice: this one
tells of traveling circus people coming into a tent for breakfast,
hard, tough, decent people, men and women riders, performers,
acrobats, clowns, jugglers, contortionists and so on, and how
they sit quietly and eat with "a savage and inspired intentness."

The food they ate was incomparably masculine and fragrant as the earth on which they wandered: it belonged to

the warm stained world of mellow sunwarmed canvas . . . and it was there for their asking with a fabulous and stupefying plenty. They ate stacks of buckwheat cakes, smoking hot, golden and embrowned, soaked in hunks of yellow butter which they carved at will . . . from the piled pints on the table, and which they garnished (if they pleased) with ropes of heavy black molasses, or with the lighter free-er maple syrup. They ate big steaks for breakfast, hot from the pan and caked with onions, they ate whole melons crammed with the ripeness of the deep pink meat, they ate thick slabs of sugared hams, rashers of bacon and great platters of fried eggs, or eggs scrambled with calves brains. . . . For their midday meal they would eat fiercely, hungrily, with wolfish gusto . . . great roasts of beef with crackled hides, browned in their juices, rare and tender, hot chunks of delicate pork with hems of fragrant fat . . . twelve pound pot roasts cooked for hours in an iron pot with new carrots, onions, sprouts, and young potatoes . . . huge roasting ears of corn, smacking hot, piled like cord-wood on two foot platters. . . .

He follows the circus people across America as they eat their way from town to town, state to state, from Maine to the Hudson and Mississippi rivers to the great plains of the West, across the prairies and north and south, from the fat farmlands of the Pennsylvania Dutch down to the Maryland shore and wheeling around the Southern states, "eating all good things that this enormous, this incredibly bountiful and abundant cornucopia of a continent yielded."

And all along the way Wolfe details what they ate, all the varieties of fish and oysters, the turtles, the cereals of the Middle West, the fat ripe fruits of Georgia and Florida, the Vermont turkeys and mountain trout, the bunched, heavy Concord grapes and winey Oregon apples, as well as

> all the clawed, the shelled, the crusted dainties, the crabs, the clams, the pink meated lobsters that grope their way along the sea-floors of America.

> —*The Good Child's River* (1935; published 1992),
> Thomas Wolfe

Now there he's serious!—and the excess fits. Where I'm amused by the earlier kitchen snacks rhapsody, this time I'm moved and he sells me every syllable because of where he's pitched his voice, speaking of hard, tough, decent people, then bringing in the broader canvas of the face and foods of the nation. Nowhere does the voice falter or strain for effects, as with "A snack!—before we prowl the meadows of the moon tonight, and soak our hearts in the moonlight's magic," or fall into Elizabethan parody as with "how sweetly doth the noble fowl submit to the swift and keen persuasion of the knife . . ." Neither passage feels worked up from notes (both Whitman and Shakespeare worked up some of their greatest descriptive passages from journals or from Plutarch or Holinshed), and amazingly, he doesn't repeat or steal from himself, although the circus passage above was cut from *Of Time and the River* and the goat-dancing snack allowed to stand.

How does he do the circus passage? What gives it its gust of power? It springs originally from his watching the circus come to town when he was a kid and being there when the stakes were driven and the big top raised, with boy Tom seeing the life behind the canvas (read his "Circus at Dawn" in *From Death to Morning*) that sets the "hard and tough" tone of real people at table. The writer's upwelling must be spoken, but this time kept to the facts. He tells of himself at age six in *Look Homeward, Angel* (1929) that he "was loose now in the limitless meadows of sensation: his sensory equipment was so complete that at the moment of perception of a single thing, the whole background of color, warmth, odor, sound, taste established itself, so that later, the breath of hot dandelion brought back the grass-warm banks of Spring, a day, a place, the rustling of young leaves, or the page of a book, the thin exotic smell of tangerine, the wintry bite of great apples . . . the spurting moments of warmth, the drip and reek of the earth-thaw, the feel of the fire." And then there was Whitman before him, with his elegy "When Lilacs Last in the Dooryard Bloom'd" and its travelogue of the great funeral train bearing Lincoln across the face of the land to Springfield. Wolfe, too, wanted to be the national bard, and here was a choice moment to show his stuff. And does he ever!

From Death to Morning is a dark book with many night passages in which Wolfe strives for a big tone, as big as anyone's, but it often sweeps from fact to fog:

> The face of the night, the heart of the dark, the tongue of the flame—I had known all things that lived or stirred or worked below her destiny. I was the child of night, a son among her mighty family, and I knew all that moved within the hearts of men who loved the night. I had seen them in a thousand places and nothing that they ever did or said was strange to me. As a child, when I had been a route boy on a morning paper, I had seen them on the streets of a little

23

town—that strange and lonely company of men who prowl the night. Sometimes they were alone, and sometimes they went together in a group of two or three, forever in mid-watches of the night in little towns prowling up and down the empty pavements of bleak streets, passing before ghastly waxen models in the windows of the clothing stores, passing below hard bulbous clusters of white light, prowling before the facades of a hundred darkened stores, pausing at length in some little lunchroom to drawl and gossip quietly, to thrust snout, lip, and sallow jowl into the stained depths of a coffee mug, or dully to wear the slow gray ash of time away without a word.

—"Death the Proud Brother," *From Death to Morning* (1935), Thomas Wolfe

When I was twenty, this passage, and many flights like it in Wolfe, knocked me flat. I came alive to the songful power of prose as never before, and spent many years imitating Wolfe's soaring ranges. But now, much older, instead of allowing Wolfe's energies to wash over me like Mahler's *Fifth,* I ask: What is it?

Well, it's fearlessly original. The first sentence bends with a curveball very hard to catch: something about destiny and night. Night is "her" and has a face, a heart, and a tongue of flame and Wolfe has known "all things that lived or stirred or worked below her destiny." Her destiny? Night's destiny? Can night have a destiny other than morning? Must words forever specify, not stir our more hidden feelings as music does?

Along with my hard time finding Wolfe's theme, the second and third sentences throw me, with "the hearts of men" becoming "them" whom this child of night has seen in a thousand places and nothing that they ever did or said was strange to him. He's seen the hearts of men doing and speaking? We know, of course, he's talking about the hearts of night prowlers and that *they* are strange and lonely and sometimes go alone or in groups of two or three, prowling up and down the empty pavements of bleak streets. This becomes spellbinding, with ghastly waxen models in clothing store windows and white-lighted street-lamps, darkened stores below "hard bulbous clusters of white light" [he means "below the hard white light of clustered bulbs," not "below hard bulbous clusters"] and a midnight lunchroom where the prowlers pause, drawl, gossip, thrust their faces into the stained depths of a coffee mug and dully "wear the slow gray ash of time away without a word"—which nicely stales the air with cigarette smoke without saying it.

Again, should we follow him so clubfootedly, image by vague image, rather than surrender to his big rhythms and dark tone, and *not* ask: What is it? He's after something under the surface of sleep and taking place in the streets and sky of our inner weathers. I make no excuses for bad writing, although Wolfe sometimes stupefies me. I'm saying he's as clear-minded as he can be about psychic events foretold by the night. And it's a good thing that he didn't give a snap for the pasting the critics gave him for *From Death to Morning*. He said he'd wait for later readers.

The big breath Wolfe draws for his hymn to the night is sucked from Whitman's great surreal night piece "The Sleepers," in which Walt is both asleep and walking about:

> *I wander all night in my vision,*
> *Stepping with light feet, swiftly and noiselessly stepping*
> *and stopping,*

Bending with open eyes over the shut eyes of sleepers,
Wandering and confused, lost to myself, ill-assorted,
contradictory,
Pausing, gazing, bending, and stopping.

How solemn they look there, stretch'd and still,
How quiet they breathe, the little children in their
cradles.

The wretched features of the ennuyes, the white features of
corpses, the livid faces of drunkards, the sick-gray
faces of onanists,
The gash'd bodies on battle-fields, the insane in their
strong-door'd room, the sacred idiots, the new-born
emerging from gates, and the dying emerging from
gates,
The night pervades and infolds them.

—"The Sleepers" (1855),
Leaves of Grass, Walt Whitman

This poem goes on for eight long sections as Whitman walks the night earth under icy "sparkles of starshine," looking down on the sleepers in their beds or graves or wards or prisons and swears they are all beautiful and makes such dream-statements as "Double yourself and receive me darkness." (What fearlessness!) Whitman slips from fact to half-dream back to fact in a way that Wolfe never tries for. Wolfe's dark Mahlerian piece, playing on his fearful joy of death, is meant to be taken musically and emotionally. Of course, Whitman does that too while still making sense and achieves many stronger effects. And,

frankly, is more moving, simply on the level of w[...]
And more daring than Wolfe, who in the past ten[...]
from his subject, while Whitman enters the [...]
dreamers, involves us in their logicless sleep lo[...]
point even finds himself deliriously running a[...]
public ("O for pity's sake, no one must see me n[...]
were stolen while I was abed,/Now I am thrust forth, where
shall I run?"), a passage still in the third edition of *Leaves of
Grass* but later cut, its humor perhaps out of tone with the rest.
Whitman remains our greatest poet of the night, maybe the
greatest night-poet ever, with such passages as this from "Song
of Myself":

> *I am he that walks with the tender and growing night,*
> *I call to the earth and sea half-held by the night.*
>
> *Press close bare-bosom'd night—press close magnetic*
> *nourishing night!*
> *Night of south winds—night of the large few stars!*
> *Still nodding night—mad naked summer night.*
>
> *Smile O voluptuous cool-breath'd earth!*
> *Earth of the slumbering and liquid trees!*
> *Earth of departed sunset—earth of the mountains misty-*
> *topt!*
> *Earth of the vitreous pour of the full moon just tinged*
> *with blue!*
> *Earth of shine and dark mottling the tide of the river!*
> *Earth of the limpid gray of clouds brighter and clearer*
> *for my sake!*

ar-swooping elbow'd earth—rich apple-blossom'd
    earth!
Smile, for your lover comes.

Prodigal, you have given me love—therefore I to you give
    love!
O unspeakable passionate love.

        —"Song of Myself" (Section 21),
        Leaves of Grass, Walt Whitman

Like Wolfe, Whitman here goes from the stepping-stone of fact to the mighty supernal cry. Remember that "the limpid gray of clouds," "Far-swooping elbow'd earth—rich apple-blossom'd earth" are washed with blue moonlight. Whitman gives a feminine charm to this immensely erotic poem by calling the night "tender and growing," "bare-bosom'd," "magnetic, nourishing," "mad naked," "voluptuous," "cool-breath'd," "slumbering and liquid," "misty-topt," "tinged with blue," with "shine and dark mottling the tide," "limpid gray . . . brighter and clearer for my sake" (the clouds are lighted from within by the moon), "far-swooping elbow'd" (that is, he's embraced by the arms of the night), "rich apple-blossom'd," and "prodigal." By prodigal he means that the night loves him with lavish extravagance, which he mirrors: "O unspeakable passionate love."

What can you say about these lines? What needs to be said? Nothing but praise. But I'll point out that the first two and last two lines frame the poem. The first two show the poet planting himself to call out to the night and get her ear in the earth and the sea half-held by the night. The two large stanzas are mad and naked as he praises her magnetic bosom and incites her voluptuousness, and—the foreplay over—they arrive at the turn, "Smile, for your lover comes." Note that "Smile" opens the third stanza, lets the stanza's argument hang fire until "Smile" repeats and closes the stanza with the turn. Once the turn is hit, the poem is over, only the adding up is needed to frame the rhapsody and with the last two lines Walt goes at once into what jazz players call the release, a few big melodic notes that swing and end the piece, delivering the lover into the body of the beloved.

Whitman mastered nineteenth-century rhetoric early: an ability to argue logically in print and in public was America's great obsession throughout his lifetime, and his ability to arrange a family of phrases in order of rising interest, then bring them to a stirring period, is shown time and again, often breathtakingly, in stanzas resounding with passion. Passion the reader fully shares, without quibbles. At times Walt's sense of rhetoric rises to a heavenly place where we don't even know we're reading rhetoric:

> *I swear they are all beautiful,*
> *Every one that sleeps is beautiful, every thing in the dim*
> *light is beautiful,*
> *The wildest and bloodiest is over, and all is peace.*

> —"The Sleepers" (Section 7),
> *Leaves of Grass,* Walt Whitman

"Beautiful," "beautiful," "beautiful," "the wildest and bloodiest," "peace." Anyone who can string three "beautifuls" together, rise to "wildest and bloodiest," and then hit that great falling note "peace" should be President of American Literature. Well, many think he is.

What I revere about Walt is that he empowers me as a man. I touch in his words a man as substantial as the sun. Feel my hand! he says, this is my soul. He's been dead a full century, but I have no trouble feeling his hand. Every morning he rises naked from his big zinc washtub, maroon all over and toweling himself, and shakes my hand as I enter his book and sneeze past the strong brown carbolic soapbar on the floor. Friend, would that you, now or a century from now, could feel my hand as I feel his in mine, and his hug, and his arm around my shoulder, draped there as he leads me to his icebox and the milk pitcher. I feel the whole weight of that arm on each page. Sure, he wrote some empty tubthumpers and dead lines, but not as many as Shakespeare. Talk about a writer who could give limbs and sensibility to your strangest thoughts alone in the woods or by yourself on the shore—that's Walt. Hey, he's not dead, I see his ribs heaving. He's just having his afternoon nap.

As with Whitman, night draws writers to itself like bridegrooms of Venus. No writer can face a night sky without a lift of joy. The night! Can it be *three years* since I've written about the night? A cry fills my hands. I'm ready, bare-bosom'd, blue-tinged, passionate night! You flow in my veins, make a sea of my arms and fingers! Wash me, beloved. And to know what a woman writer feels about the night, try this nightscape of bombed-out London:

Full moonlight drenched the city and searched it; there was not a niche left to stand in. The effect was remorseless:

London looked like the moon's capital—shallow, cratered, extinct. It was late, but not yet midnight; now the buses had stopped, the polished roads and streets in this region sent for minutes together a ghostly unbroken reflection up. The soaring new flat and the crouching old shops and houses looked equally brittle under the moon, which blazed in windows that looked its way. The futility of the black-out became laughable from the sky, presumably, you could see every slate in the roofs, every whited curb, every contour of the naked winter flowerbeds in the park; and the lake, with its shining twists and tree-darkened islands would be a landmark for miles, yes, miles, overhead.

> —"Mysterious Kor" (1944), *The Collected Stories of Elizabeth Bowen* (1981)

What fulfillment! Or rather what a kickoff. Bowen's story exists almost entirely in moonlight, aside from a flashlight and one small spotted table lamp that looks like a toadstool. The lovers, Arthur, a soldier on leave, and his racy Pepita, go to a moonlit park to make love—but it's too bright. So they go to her basement apartment which she shares with a "physically shy, brotherless virgin," Callie, who thinks herself the guardian of her friend's ideality. No sex tonight for Arthur and Pepita, whose wartime hots run high. Bowen magically unearths the depths of these three in the darkness of their blacked-out apartment, much like an archaeologist digging in "Mysterious Kor," a lost city whose buildings still stand. Cratered London by moonlight is now extinct Kor and the anxieties of air bombardment strip these three naked as they would seldom be stripped in peacetime. People stay indoors with a fervor that can be felt:

31

the buildings strain with battened-down human life, "but not a beam, not a voice, not a note from a radio escaped."

What prints the story forever in memory is Bowen's use of moonlight throughout, with eerie white moonlight popping up naturally but surprisingly everywhere. Even the waterbirds in the park have been wakened by the moon. Before the lovers arrive for the night, Callie sees what she thinks is a blue-white searchlight beam on her blackout curtains, parts them slowly, looks out—and is face-to-face with the moon.

Below the moon the houses opposite her window blazed back in transparent shadow; and something—was it a coin or a ring?—glittered halfway across the chalk-white street. . . . Having drunk in the white explanation, Callie lay down again. Her half of the bed was in shadow, but she allowed one hand to lie, blanched, in what should be Pepita's place. She lay and looked at the hand until it was no longer her own.

It's *A Midsummer Night's Dream* for wartime, with many tart moments, and an inspired ending that could as well be on the moon.

How does she do it? Well, she follows Keats's advice to Shelley, "load every rift with ore": listen to the two richest words in the first sentence, "drenched" and "niche"—Keats smiles and nods at that: "A prosperous beginning, Bowen." But she also has "searched," or two *ch* sounds that lead to a soft *sh*, to give the texture and impact of full moonlight on London, with the softer "niche" loading the rifts between buildings with blazing ore. And she quickly goes on with "*sh*allow" and poli*sh*ed," so that by the time we get to Callie at the blackout curtain we get "*sh*adow" again, "glittered," "*ch*alk-white" and the hallucinatory "Her half of the bed was in *sh*adow, but *sh*e allowed one hand to lie, blan*ch*ed, in what *sh*ould be Pepita's place. *Sh*e lay and looked at the hand until it was no longer her own." With Callie spellbound by the searchlight moon and a hypnotic coin or ring glittering in the chalk-white street, we know why her fugue state and blanched hand "no longer her own" have Keats dancing with Coleridge.

Summers I spend on Cape Cod, and with a few minutes' walk can reach the bare dunes where the house Henry Beston once lived in has washed away. He wrote a cosmic memoir about a year he spent alone on Nauset Beach in the outermost house on the continental United States. He wrote in longhand on the kitchen table, at night by candlelight or lamp, looking out at the North Atlantic and the dunes, "the paths of the channels stilled to twilight bronze." Here he describes night on the great beach:

> I went down to the beach that night just after ten o'clock. So utterly black, pitch dark it was, and so thick with moisture and trailing showers, that there was no sign whatever of the beam of Nauset; the sea was only a sound, and when I reached the edge of the surf the dunes themselves had disappeared behind. I stood as isolate in that immensity of rain and night as I might have stood in interplanetary space. The sea was troubled and noisy, and when I opened the darkness with an outlined cone of light from my electric torch I saw that the waves were washing up green coils of sea grass, all coldly wet and bright in the motionless and unnatural radiance. Far off a single ship was groaning its way along the

shoals. The fog was compact of the finest moisture; passing by, it spun itself into my lens of light like a kind of strange, aerial and liquid silk. . . .

—"On the Great Beach," *The Outermost House* (1928), Henry Beston

Well done and imaginative as this is, its phrasing could be better. I like the whole, its mood, and superb detail. I like less the voice, though its honesty refreshes. Here's how he might have written it today, sixty-four years later (he wrote his book the year I was born):

I went down to the beach that night just after ten o'clock. Utterly black, the night lay thick with fine dampness and trailing showers. No sign whatever of the beam from Nauset. The sea sounded heavily. When I reached the edge of the surf the dunes themselves fled, lost in mist. I stood as alone in that immensity of rain and night as if on a rock in outer space. The sea spoke, harsh and noisy, and when I lanced open the darkness with my flashlight beam, I saw waves washing up green coils of eelgrass and sea lace. The stiff unnatural radiance of my beam picked its cold way into the bright angry fall of each grassy wave. Far off a single ship groaned its way along the shoals. The fine-spun fog passed by my lens, a strange, aerial, liquid silk. . . .

I make no claims for this, only that a straightforward sentence can sing as strongly as his old-fashioned turns of speech. You may think that digging your way through his line deepens the experience, and, in fact, that his voice is pitched to a higher

34

muse than mine, that he draws more from the reader with his passive voicings than I do with active verbs. I defend nothing, only tell you how I rewrite everyone when I read—and retongue all Latin into Anglo-Saxon.

Norman Mailer writes about living above the Cape surf this way:

> At dawn, if it was low tide on the flats, I would awaken to the chatter of gulls. On a bad morning, I used to feel as if I had died and the birds were feeding on my heart. Later, after I dozed for a while, the tide would come up over the sand as swiftly as a shadow descends on the hills when the sun lowers behind the ridge, and before long the first swells would pound on the bulkhead of the deck below my bedroom window, the shock rising in one fine fragment of time from the sea wall to the innermost passages of my flesh. *Boom!* the waves would go against the wall, and I could have been alone on a freighter on a dark sea.
>
> —*Tough Guys Don't Dance* (1984), Norman Mailer

Mailer's grip tightens, weaves us into his melodrama. He decides not to pitch his first paragraph in a higher voice or promise us more than he plans to give. This is a mystery, not a cosmic workout. Let the events make their own deeper notes.

Melville finds himself richly amused by the surly Ishmael's arrival in New Bedford, as Ishmael wanders about looking for a night's lodging before catching the next night's ferry to Nantucket:

> With halting steps I paced the streets, and passed the sign of "The Crossed Harpoons"—but it looked too expensive

and jolly there. Further on, from the bright red windows of the "Sword-Fish Inn," there came such fervent rays, that it seemed to have melted the packed snow and ice from before the house, for everywhere else the congealed frost lay ten inches thick in a hard, asphaltic pavement,—rather weary for me, when I struck my foot against the flinty projections, because from hard, remorseless service the soles of my boots were in a most miserable plight. Too expensive and jolly, again thought I, pausing one moment to watch the broad glare in the street, and hear the sounds of the tinkling glasses within. But go on, Ishmael, said I at last; don't you hear? get away from before the door; your patched boots are stopping the way. So on I went. I now by instinct followed the streets that took me waterward, for there, doubtless, were the cheapest, if not the cheeriest inns.

Such dreary streets! blocks of blackness, not houses, on either hand, and here and there a candle, like a candle moving about in a tomb. At this hour of the night, of the last day of the week, that quarter of the town proved all but deserted. But presently I came to a smoky light proceeding from a low, wide building, the door of which stood invitingly open. It had a careless look, as if it were meant for the uses of the public; so, entering, the first thing I did was to stumble over an ash-box in the porch. Ha! thought I, ha, as the flying particles almost choked me, are these ashes from that destroyed city, Gomorrah? But "The Crossed Harpoons," and "The Sword-Fish"?—this, then, must needs be the sign of "The Trap." However, I picked myself up and hearing a loud voice within, pushed on and opened a second, interior door.

It seemed the great Black Parliament sitting in Tophet. A hundred black faces turned round in their rows to peer; and beyond, a black Angel of Doom was beating a book in a pulpit. It was a negro church; and the preacher's text was about the blackness of darkness, and the weeping and wailing and teeth-gnashing there. Ha, Ishmael, muttered I, backing out, Wretched entertainment at the sign of "The Trap"!

—*Moby-Dick* (1851), Herman Melville

I've remembered those dreary New Bedford streets since first reading about them in my youth, when I took all this scene-setting with deep-soaked seriousness as if working my way through a whole plum pudding thick with nuts and raisins. That Melville is laughing behind Ishmael's mishaps never struck me. But his amusement is clear in Ishmael's Popeye-like murky mutterings and natterings about the inns being too jolly and in the pinchpurse schoolmaster likening the ash-box to Gomorrah. Recall that in the famous first paragraph Ishmael decides to go whaling rather than commit suicide. *I yam what I yam and that's what I yam*—Ishmael, the existential sailorman.

Perhaps you have to type this up yourself, as I've just done, to hear Melville nicker through his mask of Ishmael. When you type it, you are Melville and slowly gather your story into coils, inn by inn and block by block, and the pricking of Ishmael's holed soles by flinty ice and his kicking the ash-box with its flying particles as he looks for a less cheerful inn (remember, the dreary streets are already "blocks of blackness, not houses," with here and there a candle moving about as if in a tomb), well, this pricking and kicking sink you into a blackness with Ishmael. Melville's mouth waters to sketch in charcoal the spiritual night-state of his storyteller who walks on ten-inch-thick ice through black New Bedford and stumbles at last into the

37

smoky Black Parliament of a Bible-beating black preacher. This "blackness of darkness" scene, of course, balances the "Whiteness of the Whale" chapter. Typing, I felt the ice on my footsoles and felt the very ashes in the ash-box fly into my eye, as did Melville. And what a dreary ass I used to be, reading this all so solemnly, sniffing each line for great phrases of candied fruit. I deserved no "tinkling glasses" or bright red windows' fervent rays. Call me Ishmael.

Here are two Cape Cod beach pieces from a novel-in-progress by my wife, Nancy. She'd made notes for this book since the 1950s, then actually sat down to compose sixteen years ago. It's a portmanteau novel and she sticks into it anything she wants to from life. She's now reordering chapters and shaping it. In the novel's first paragraphs the heroine, Mary, recalls her childhood:

I had on a blue wool bathing suit. As it dried it smelled strongly of sea. It had a square front and crossed straps in back that striped my skin white when Mother took it off. My sisters were swimming in the crystal green Atlantic. I crouched in sand that blazed like fool's gold in Cape light. I was digging a hole with my red tin shovel that bent at the neck.

My father got up from the indigo plaid spread where Mother sat. He went back to our bayfront cottage behind the shining grass. He came back with a big garden spade.

"Let's dig a hole," he said. "If we dig very deep, we'll get to China!"

He put his foot on the spade and we started for China. He had on white pants and a blowing white shirt. He was laughing and I believed him. We dug until moonlight when Mother called.

I like the old photo effect of the first paragraph, with its primary Kodacolors from the thirties and the past tense lending a slightly aged quality. Everything in this passage springs from a child's senses, the crystal green Atlantic, the blaze of sand, the shining grass, the seasmell of her dried suit, and strengthens Mary's artless trust that her father is digging a hole to China.

In the second piece Mary is fifteen and with her first boyfriend, Scott, with whom she has intense ties for over nine years:

At the end of August, the Yacht Club held its last dance. The band played "Don't Get Around Much Anymore" and I whirled in my white cotton dress as the salt night air poured in through doors and open windows. I felt his hand and smelled his cheek and could not stop each moment as it passed.

During intermission we leaned on a rail and I threw a bit of sand into the water. Its spray stirred mineral deeps and phosphorescent star-flowers bloomed in a black sea, twin universe of the star-impacted sky above. It was the same night sky I'd behold years later from my Cape Cod meadow, eyes unmoving from the blazing lights of August as a second marriage crumbled round me. The same night sky that later still, blasted rosy silver by an aurora borealis, shined as I lay in the grass at last with Byron. The same night sky that years earlier, to beat back my ten-year-old's terror of the dark, my father pointed to on our long walks around the hills of our home. He'd speak with awe about the constellations, the galaxies. We'd find the dippers, Orion, Venus, and he'd tell me there was a God—he knew it—He'd answered his prayers many times. The panic in my body would fade as I shared the blessing of the cosmos with my father who loved the sky and remembered his own boyhood in Armenia (real estate claimed by the Turks) where he lay long summer nights on a clay roof and watched "an apricot moon as big as a table top, Mary," rise among big chips of low-hanging stars in the fiery midnight blue of Asia Minor.

I loved Scott with a longing that would not stop for years. It just dimmed.

—*The Banqueting House* (forthcoming), Nancy Newlove

Not born on Cape Cod, I am what the natives call a "washed ashore," as in "he just washed ashoah twenty years ago," and my wife had to explain to me that a pinch of sand dropped into seawater at night gives rise to a mineral phosphorescence. In something of the same here, she drops grains into the night sky and brings into bloom phosphors of feeling. I enjoy deeply the bony fifteen-year-old at her last Yacht Club dance with Scott, then the sky as a diary of "Mary's" marriages (all her husbands and lovers are named Byron), and her night terrors as a child, which her father allayed by pointing out the constellations and telling of God answering his prayers. Then come her father's words about the moon against low-hanging big chips, seen as a boy from his clay roof in Armenia, "an apricot moon as big as a table top, Mary," which rides on the bass note of "the fiery midnight blue of Asia Minor"—how far from this Yacht Club dance! All these details carry the theme of time's onrush, none are extra, and Mary rounds them out with her confession of unwavering fealty to Scott despite the dimming of time.

I delight in those big chips of stars and that apricot moon by my in-house critic. Beat me, if you must, for including her.

No midcentury western writer brought the western night to life more crisply than Louis L'Amour, who could pull moon-shadows across the bright-clouded prairie like few others. His characters rise up out of landscape. In this night passage, you can't tell the cowboy from his saddle or the sagebrush:

> We started up Coyote Creek in the late hours of the night, with stars hanging their bright lanterns over the mountains. Cap was riding point, our six pack horses trailing him, and me riding drag. A chill wind came down off the Sangre de Cristos, and somewhere out over the bottom a quail was calling. . . .
>
> We circled around the sleeping village of Golondrinos, and pointed north, shivering in the morning cold. The sky was stark and clear, the ridges sharply cut against the faintly lightening sky. Grass swished about our horses' hoofs, our saddles creaked, and over at Golondrinos a dog barked inquiringly into the morning.
>
> —*Sackett* (1961), Louis L'Amour

Only a man as hard as dirt can live like this. You can't help wanting to copy L'Amour's magnetic simplicity and have your own grass swish and dog bark inquiringly into the morning. In the first paragraph the plosive *p*'s and hard *k*'s and the broad *a*'s of "hanging," "trailing," "Cap," "pack," "drag," "came," "Sangre," and "quail" impact you into hardsaddle life in a chill wind under the bright lanterns.

He rounds out the second passage with sound-imagery just

as he did the first, not with a quail calling but with a swish, a creak, "and over at Golondrinos a dog barked inquiringly into the morning." The dog bark imagery spreads Homerically across the mind because the long line suggests the flatness of the land while the drawl of "over at Golondrinos a dog" and the two *ing*s of "inquir*ing*ly" and "morn*ing*" stretch the line, which ends not with a hard syllable but a lingering feminine fall on morn*ing* that carries the dog bark to the edges of imagination. Mmm, a well-turned line shivers me real nice.

Jane Tompkins's study of westerns in *West of Everything* shows her to be a big L'Amour fan, and I steal her quotes from *Sackett:*

> I walked my horse across a high meadow that lay beyond the curtain of trees. The ground was nigh covered by alpine gold-flower, bright yellow, and almighty pretty to look at. And along some of the trickles running down from the melting snow a kind of primrose was growing.
>
> The trees were mostly blue spruce, shading off into aspen and, on the high ridges above timberline, there were a few squat bristle-cone pines, gnarled from their endless war with the wind.
>
> A couple of times I found where whoever it was I was trailing had stopped to pick some kind of herb out of the grass, or to drink at a stream.

This artless voice—"Poetry? Don't know much about it!"—weighs each detail like John Donne beating gold to an "aery thinness." Blow on that almighty pretty first paragraph and the words float off like dandelion fluff. You can practically pick that primrose, or see a hole in the stream where the man he's trailing drank.

Rhyming "trickles" and "a kind of primrose," the beautiful lisp of "blue spruce," "aspen," "squat bristle-cone pines, gnarled from their endless war with the wind"—that's some ear.

Like Louis L'Amour, Raymond Chandler, an intensely poetic stylist, began in pulps and became a touchstone for excellence. No one matched his descriptions of Los Angeles until Joan Didion fled New York for rebirth in the Golden Land. His first novel, *The Big Sleep,* became a film noir classic second only to *The Maltese Falcon.* This passage, the novel's fade-out, gives a landscape of Philip Marlowe's mind as he leaves the mansion of the dying millionaire who hired him, now knowing that the body of Rusty Regan lies deep in a sump:

I went quickly away from her down the room and out and down the tiled staircase to the front hall. I didn't see anybody when I left. I found my hat alone this time. Outside, the bright gardens had a haunted look, as though small wild eyes were watching me from behind the bushes, as though the sunshine itself had a mysterious something in its light. I got into my car and drove off down the hill.

What did it matter where you lay once you were dead? In a dirty sump or in a marble tower on top of a high hill? You were dead, you were sleeping the big sleep, you were not bothered by things like that. Oil and water were the same as wind and air to you. You just slept the big sleep, not caring about the nastiness of how you died or where you fell. Me, I was part of the nastiness now. Far more a part of it than Rusty Regan was. But the old man didn't have to be. He could lie quiet in his canopied bed, with his bloodless hands folded on the sheet, waiting. His heart was a brief, uncertain murmur. His thoughts were as gray as ashes. And in a little while he too, like Rusty Regan, would be sleeping the big sleep.

—The Big Sleep (1939), Raymond Chandler

Why's this memorable? The voice. Marlowe could have said anything and still the novel would end like a dog chewing on its own leg. But Chandler lucked onto his title phrase and today the whole story takes place in a big sleep. The Humphrey Bogart film version, directed by Howard Hawks from a script by William Faulkner, Jules Furthman and Leigh Brackett, remains so perversely, even magnificently mixed up that few can follow it, and even Chandler himself couldn't name who murdered the chauffeur, in the movie or the novel. Talk about a big sleep.

What makes this ending work? Well, first we're given a string of purposefully colorless camera shots—"away from," "down," "out," "down," "to"—to move us downstairs but also to lower our guard. We're going to our execution. Once outside, Marlowe's struck by a haunted look to the bright gardens, "as though small wild eyes were watching me from behind the bushes," and even more disorienting, "as though the sunshine itself had a mysterious something in its light." (Scotch, maybe?) Chandler sets up his magical, even gorgeous estrangement before pulling on a black hood for the guillotine blade of his grand phrase.

Our necks in place, he goes straight into his chopping block aria: "What did it matter where you lay once you were dead? In a dirty sump or in a marble tower on top of a high hill?" It's Cio-Cio San singing "One Fine Day," pure Puccini, only the words are "You were dead, you were sleeping the big sleep, you were not bothered by things like that. *Oil-l and water-r were the same as wind and air to you!* You just slept the big sleep, not caring about the nastiness of how you died or where you fell. . . ."

And in a little while we too will sleep the big sleep, for Chandler's comic theme is the vanity and worthlessness of human works, even solving a crime. Marlowe, chock-full of fun, makes up literary chat in a way no detective ever talked. In the first scene, attacked by a nymphomaniac, he gets off some zingers and seldom lets up for the rest of the novel, unless action or great tension arises. His futility aria is sublime fun, though few readers take it as such. Its tone is perfection, given the story, and shows his characters as so many dancing dogs. He's *not* serious.

When a writer's really serious about the emptiness of human life, he doesn't laugh. He gives us horror in his deepest voice, as does another Marlow, the storyteller of Joseph Conrad's *Heart of Darkness,* who tells us about his trip up the Congo:

Going up the river was like travelling back to the earliest beginnings of the world, when vegetation rioted on the earth and the big trees were kings. An empty stream, a great silence, an impenetrable forest. The air was warm, thick, heavy, sluggish. There was no joy in the brilliance of sunshine. The long stretches of the waterway ran on, deserted, into the gloom of over-shadowed distances. On silvery sandbanks hippos and alligators sunned themselves side by side. The broadening waters flowed through a mob of wooded islands; you lost your way on that river as you would in a desert, and butted all day long against shoal, trying to find the channel, till you thought yourself bewitched and cut off for ever from everything you had known once—somewhere—far away—in another existence perhaps. There were moments when one's past came back to one, as it will sometimes when you have not a moment to spare to yourself, but it came in the shape of an unrestful and noisy dream, remembered with wonder amongst the overwhelming realities of this strange world of plants, and water, and silence. And this stillness of life did not in the least resemble a peace. It was the stillness of an implacable force brooding over an inscrutable intention. It looked at you with a vengeful aspect. I got used to it afterwards; I did not see it any more; I had no time. I had to keep guessing at the channel; I had to discern, mostly by inspiration, the signs of hidden banks; I watched for sunken stones; I was learning to clap my teeth smartly before my heart flew out, when I shaved by a fluke some infernal old snag that would have ripped the life out of the tin-pot steamboat and drowned all the pilgrims; I had to keep a look-out for the signs of dead wood we could cut up in the night for next day's steaming. When you have to attend to things of that sort, to the mere incidents of the surface, the reality—the reality, I tell you—fades. The inner truth is hidden—luckily, luckily. But I felt it all the same; I felt often its mysterious stillness watching me at my monkey tricks, just as it watches you fellows performing on your respective tight-ropes for—what is it? half a crown a tumble—

—*Heart of Darkness* (1902), Joseph Conrad

Heart of Darkness is a book for slow readers who savor each phrase of rising horror as it echoes from passage to passage. The tale is largely description, so landscape is action. The horror that Marlow steams into the heart of floods the overgrowth and runs down his back in the clamp of warm, thick, heavy, slug-gish air.

Marlow tells this story one long afternoon to four men sitting on a yacht anchored on the Thames, and it's about his going up the Congo to find Mr. Kurtz, an ivory trader who seems to have gone native, and gone mad as well. Right at the top, Marlow gives his big tune to the bass fiddles: "Going up the river was like travelling back to the earliest beginnings of the world, when vegetation rioted on the earth and the big trees were kings." With a theme and variations on big trees and rioting vegetation, Marlow, or Conrad, knows he has to get a proper glitter in his eye if he is to run his nails over our imaginations and light up our nervous systems with his terrible news about the basic savagery of man. And this news isn't merely philosophical—it's a dead bird stuck in his gullet. Mostly he chooses simple words to keep up tension. But "impenetrable," "implacable," and "inscrutable" should go. I'd like "unpierceable forest," much weirder and fresher than "impenetrable forest," and later "the stillness of a stonefaced and unreadable force," not "an implacable force brooding over an inscrutable intention." A *"force"* brooding over an *"intention"*? That's mumbo jumbo, though its shadowy hint of "brooding" evil being part of nature, a psychic growth as real as the air and vines, takes us deeply into Marlow's agonized discovery: that his journey led him out of the illusions of society and into an inhuman blackness of nature and of man himself, an idea sold here with civilized "Mistah Kurtz" stripped to his savage beginnings. But would Marlow unload such vague high claptrap as "the stillness of an implacable force brooding over an inscrutable intention" on his four listeners? Not without blushing.

Even vegetation rioting is a garden journal commonplace, and the big trees as kings of rioting vegetation a cartoon. Can you hear Hemingway tell about an Africa "when vegetation rioted on the earth and the big trees were kings"—or say that even about the beginning of the world? But enough. I love this paragraph! Conrad's not writing adventure or travel prose, he's digging down for the actual sensations and weirdness of a real trip he took up the Congo and which aged him right out of his youth. That he's wrapping all this around a tale told by Marlow is fun, but what moves me is Conrad himself, behind his Marlow mask, taking his own pulse as he relives the past—and shudders. He's not miming fancy English writers, this is his own blood guttering through the images.

What works is just about everything. We move upriver into a great silence. Compare this Marlow's "There was no joy in the brilliance of sunshine" with Philip Marlowe's "Outside, the bright gardens had a haunted look . . . as though the sunshine itself had a mysterious something in its light." Has Marlowe been reading Marlow? Well, haunted sunshine?—it's a staple of horror stories, as old as the fourteenth century's *Sir Gawain and the Green Knight,* and befits Marlowe's knight-errantry in high California brilliance as much as Marlow's sun-drenched Congo errand. With Conrad, we see a lot more than we smell or hear. Conrad had an artistic rule: "before all, to make you *see*" and make plain to the reader's eye the moral truth of his story. Conrad really believes this story; it's short but it's his *King Lear,* man seen at his worst, not just thumbing out old men's eyes but impaling heads on stakes. When Marlow tells us about the first of many heads he saw on poles in front of Kurtz's ruined house, we are sure that Conrad has woven into Marlow's shock something once seen by himself in the Congo: "... and there it was, black, dried, sunken, with closed eyelids—a head that seemed to sleep at the top of that pole, and, with the shrunken dry lips showing a narrow white line of the teeth, was smiling too, smiling continuously at some endless and jocose dream of that eternal slumber." Terrific, that narrow white line of teeth smiling between shrunken dry lips, a smile that bites into Conrad's deepest feelings, though "jocose" and "eternal slumber" are literary slumming. Smiling to himself like a Halloween prankster, an inspired Conrad has saved in his heart and silently savored and worked up to this dried head since the start of his story, and the smile on its teeth is at the heart of his own darkness, "an unrestful and noisy dream, remembered with wonder ..." *Boy!* And don't skim over Marlow's great nightmarish detail about hidden banks and sunken stones: "... I was learning to clap my teeth smartly before my heart flew out ..."

Who else has been listening to Marlow? How about this night scene from Robert Stone's *Outerbridge Reach*. Before setting forth on a yacht to attempt to sail around the world alone, Owen Browne takes a last look at New Jersey from "the twilight shadows of the Upper Bay" from aboard the *Parsifal* (or Holy Fool):

The gathered night was starless and soiled by the glow of the harbor. Red and white refinery lights dappled the surface of the water. The wind carried the stench of the Fresh Kills dump. He ducked below and jammed a tape into the machine. The voice of Russ Colombo wafted into the sour-smelling darkness. "I Couldn't Sleep a Wink Last Night" was the song. With his tape at full volume, he eased past the Island of Meadow. His lights caught a rat running along the oily bank of the Jersey shore. Then he saw another. He shivered in the wintry breeze that had come up with darkness.

Ahead of him were the lights of the bridge that spanned the Kill. When he saw the black derelict shapes of a salvage yard on the Staten Island shore, he turned in and cut the motor.

In a still backwater off the Kill, ringed with lights like a prison yard, wooden tugs and ferries were scattered like a child's toy boats. Some lay half submerged and gutted, their stacks and steam engines moldering beside them in the shallows. Others were piled on each other four and five high, in dark masses that towered above the water. . . . The wooden boats that rotted there, floodlit and girded round with electrified fence and razor wire, had been working harbor craft eighty and ninety years before. . . .

Parsifal's port float ran up the hull plates of a decaying tug, raising the shriek of fiberglass on metal. Under the awful sound, Russ Colombo's seamless crooning sounded on. The tug lay so far over that Browne could step out onto her topsides. He threw a line around a bitt on the tug's fo'c'sle and secured it. Then he walked along the rust-flaked hull to the wheelhouse and hunkered down to look around him. Somewhere ashore, a dog began to bark.

On Browne's left, the hulks lay scattered in a geometry of shadows. The busy sheer and curve of their shapes and the perfect stillness of the water made them appear held fast in some phantom disaster. Across the Kill, bulbous storage tanks, generators and floodlit power lines stretched to the end of darkness. The place was marked on the charts as Out-erbridge Reach.

—*Outerbridge Reach* (1992), Robert Stone

I abridge this by cutting plotto about Browne's stepfather owning the tug dump. The likeness to *Heart of Darkness* in *Outerbridge Reach* is that here seascape is action, or rather seagoing detail is. Both writers have the same goal, to convince us of something haunted in the landscape. Conrad tells us straight out, Stone suggests through his Boschian detail of the red and white refinery lights, the darkness, the black derelict shapes, the shore rats, the "starless and soiled" night sky, the shivering wintry breeze, the half-sunken and gutted wooden tugs and ferries "ringed with lights like a prison yard," moldering steam engines, boats in dark masses "piled on each other four and five high," their floodlit rotting and electrified fence girded with razor wire, the shriek of fiberglass on metal as the *Parsifal* runs up the rust-flaked hull plates of a decaying tug, the "phantom disaster" and so on. These wooden boats, harbor craft eighty and ninety years old, are now hulks "scattered in a geometry of shadows." And, of course, their fate foretells or at least warns us of what may happen to Browne, who faces a dreadful time in his own geometry of shadows.

This big, dark passage is my favorite in the novel (think of Stone as that barking dog). When Browne's fate at last comes down on him, it's spread out over several chapters and none have a compression and richness to match this foreshadowing, perhaps because his fate arrives only bit by bit as his mind flakes and decays. No matter. What does happen to Browne is plenty scary. Does the holy fool seeking rebirth prove spiritually worthy? Find out for yourself.

Stone creates the seagoing parts of his story largely out of detail. In the passage above, the nautical detail quite likely outstrips the reader's knowledge while Stone keeps his strength up by knowing more than the reader about what he's telling him. In Conrad the conviction that we are under steam up the Congo relies much less on sailcraft than on the sense of entering a hallucination in which all detail is equally dream-ridden. Stone's details glow with a queasy light. When Browne is at last alone at sea, yachting terms sticker the paragraphs and stand in place of a stronger adversary for Browne to strive against when not striving with himself. I carp that these terms are padding and that Stone lets the reader paddle in place while waiting for the next gust in the story. Stone himself, never having set forth to sail around the globe, can draw only on imagination and sea and sky and yachting terms to keep afloat or fend off a windless passage. At times his invention is tremendous, as with a variety of surreal signals Browne keeps getting on his shortwave band, and with a creepily drawn haunted house he finds on a deserted island. It's no crime to be less compelling than *Heart of Darkness*.

(One stupid carp: As a Russ Colombo fan, I just gotta say that Colombo—who died in 1934—could not be crooning "I Couldn't Sleep a Wink Last Night," a song by Jimmy McHugh and Harold Adamson for Frank Sinatra's 1943 debut starrer *Higher and Higher*. Now I hear Sinatra when I read this passage when I'd rather hear Russ crooning "Just Friends" or "Time on My Hands.")

Now, look at this night scene from Stone's earlier novel *A*

Flag for Sunrise, which is set in a fictional Central American country. A thoroughly drunken Lieutenant Campos decides that he has sinned, wants to confess, and with "insane intelligent eyes smoldering in the moonlight" drives Father Egan, a rummy priest, to Campos's bungalow, gives him two glasses of rum, then opens the top door of a red freezer and stands by it with a face full of "stoic grief":

Fearfully, Egan followed the lieutenant's gaze and saw that the freezer contained an unplucked turkey and a great many bottles of Germania beer. Beneath them was a bolt of green cloth. Puzzled, he turned to Campos but the lieutenant had closed his eyes and was biting his lip, as though to control his emotions. Egan reached down, moved a few of the bottles of frozen beer and his eye fell on the maple-leaf flag of Canada. . . .

He scanned the surface contents of the chest, amorphous cubes of ice, the enormous turkey, the bottles of beer with their peeling labels, and saw at last—in one corner, partially concealed by ice—a human foot. Looking more closely he saw that it curved downward from a turned ankle on which there was a small cut gone black. The outer side of the foot was visible, its callused edge pressed against the top of a South American sandal. The thong of the sandal divided the darkly veined front of the foot; caught between two of the toes was a tiny cotton pompon of bright red. Father Egan looked down at the foot and understood only its beautiful symmetry, its functional wholeness, the sublime engineering that had appended its five longish toes. The top of it, he saw, was suntanned.

Then his knees buckled under him. As he reached out

to steady himself, his hand clawed across the ice cubes and revealed a moist matting of yellow hair, then a tanned forehead. Then below, the freckled bridge of a nose and an eye—blue with foliate iris—the whites gone dark, an eye so dull, so dead with sheer animal death that Egan received the sight of it as a spiritual shock.

He staggered back from the ice chest.

—*A Flag for Sunrise* (1981), Robert Stone

Here is dreadful intensity. For Father Egan finds, jackknifed into the chest, a young blond girl in khaki shorts, her Boy Scout shift bearing a maple-leaf flag. Stone draws out the opening, keeps withholding the horror of the lieutenant's secret, lets it crawl to the spine-shaking freckled bridge of a nose and foliate iris. First, though, he draws us into the priest studying the freezer's enormous unplucked turkey. The bare flesh of a *plucked* turkey might shock us needlessly ahead of time, so this big bird is unplucked and frozen in its feathers. There's the strange bolt of green cloth—her head scarf?—and the weird Campos, biting his lip, struggles with his feelings.

Then Stone starts giving us the foot. Slowly. It has a small ankle cut gone black. Its callused edge presses against a sandal. The foot is darkly veined. Two toes hold a tiny pompon of bright red. How beautiful this foot, functional, whole, and its "sublime engineering . . . had appended its five longish toes." The top is suntanned.

Then Stone bops us and the priest's knees buckle. He claws across ice cubes, finds a moist matting of yellow hair, then a tanned forehead. And then, wham, eye and iris.

My only question about that single eye is why the "whites"

54

have gone dark, not the "white." "Whites" suggests a second eye. A typo?

The scene goes on brilliantly with the lieutenant demanding to be confessed and absolved by the priest. Aside from the Graham Greene stuff about this drunken priest having the power of Christ, which reminds us strongly of the alcoholic Mexican priest in *The Power and the Glory* (1940), what makes this passage so original? We sense Stone questioning himself at depth about his effects and dramatizing his own spiritual horror in the face of an insane act which has placed this darkening girl in a red freezer. The turkey and bottles of Germania beer are just so much trimming to the dehumanized creature in South American sandals, though why South American sandals, rather than Central American, is a subtlety I can't speak to.

How does this scene stand up against Browne's ghastly visit to Outerbridge Reach? Both strike many of the same notes in us. But where each is placed means much. Browne's scene comes a third of the way into *Outerbridge Reach* and we have waited hard for that chord to be struck. And it fulfills itself. Browne is not a man who questions himself deeply, but the ships' graveyard warns him of a spiritual state possibly soon to be his. He carries the rats and rust and fear of that soiled place with him to sea. Before novel's end he must face Outerbridge Reach in himself, thousands of miles away from the soiled tug dump.

The iced girl scene kicks off the first chapter of *A Flag for Sunrise*. When I heard Stone give a reading from the novel as a work in progress, this scene was not first. Later, he chose to set his hook into the reader good and deep and lead with this spellbinder. A wise choice!—charging the reader's imagination with an experience he or she will never forget. Aside from the horror, the scene asks the novel's deepest question, what to do when all human illusion is stripped away—and the rest of the story works variations on this theme. At novel's end, after horror upon horror, we are told, "The absence of evil is the greatest horror."

Here is how Hemingway handles a scene by water with hints of horror. Young Nick Adams has just returned from the war in Italy and, to replenish his soul, gone fishing alone in the country. The war is never mentioned, nor is his war wound, but they're suggested by Nick's opening description of the landscape at Horton's Bay, the logging camp where he begins his trip inland to his favorite trout stream. A hillside at Horton's Bay, blackened by fire, stands psychically for World War I. All the grasshoppers in the region are black with soot, giving us a sense of the natural world itself fallen into disaster. But, Nick thinks, in time the grasshoppers will be green again, even as Nick will be restored. We watch him set up camp, mix some canned spaghetti and beans for supper, then lay down to sleep for the night. The next day he fishes the stream until he's tired. Hemingway's details of trout fishing are as masterful as Turgenev's or Tolstoy's and avoid any exaggeration about fishing or the sense of a trout pulling on the reader's own wrists as Nick tries to keep his light line and rod from snapping. His catch, still alive in a sack around his waist, beats on the reader's thigh.

Ahead the river narrowed and went into a swamp. The river became smooth and deep and the swamp looked solid with cedar trees, their trunks close together, their branches solid. It would not be possible to walk through a swamp like that. The branches grew so low. You would have to keep almost level with the ground to move at all. You could not crash through the branches. That must be why the animals that lived in swamps were built the way they were . . .

Nick did not want to go in there now. He felt a reaction against deep wading with the water deepening up under his armpits, to hook big trout in places impossible to land them. In the swamp the banks were bare, the big cedars came together overhead, the sun did not come through, except in patches; in the fast deep water, in the half light, the fishing would be tragic. In the swamp fishing was a tragic adventure. Nick did not want it. He did not want to go down the stream any further today. . . .

Nick stood up on the log, holding his rod, the landing net hanging heavy, then stepped into the water and splashed ashore. He climbed the bank and cut up into the woods, toward the high ground. He was going back to camp. He looked back. The river just showed through the trees. There were plenty of days coming when he could fish the swamp.

—"Big Two-Hearted River: Part II" (1924), *The Complete Short Stories of Ernest Hemingway,* Finca Vigia edition

I have—not without pain!—gutted this passage of its glorious detail about fish and highlighted the tragic darkness that Hemingway wants us to sense below the surface of his story. This story must be read twice, at least, to begin to fathom. I know how tiresome and unclear it was for me on first reading, much like a Cubist painting you at first can't grasp—why does he go on and on with all this description? But like that painting it swims together at last and delights you. "Big Two-Hearted River" is my favorite Hemingway short story and for me its tragic quality sings throughout. Aside from the burnt-over Horton's Bay hillside, other details of natural disaster include Nick wetting his hand when unhooking an undersize trout—he does not want to disturb the thick mucus on the fish and has seen too many trout die of fungus after being handled with dry fingers. A big trout breaks his line and he knows the fish is down deep and very angry about the hook in its jaw. He does not *tell* us about the fish's pain—he doesn't have to. The log under which he finds a nest of sooty grasshoppers and selects a jarful of middle-sized insects reminds us of *King Lear*'s "We are as flies to the gods." A log on which he strikes a match is rotting and he must seek out a hard place to strike the match. Rot is natural. We watch him break the necks of two trout, then neatly gut them. A psychic detail here is that they are both males, with long gray-white strips of milt. Hemingway himself had lost a testicle when wounded in Italy, a wound whose pain he later takes much further by having Jake Barnes, his hero in *The Sun Also Rises,* lose his cock in the war—though not his hormones. Hemingway's wound in no way shrank his sex life—but it made him thoughtful, and the stripped-out milt darkens the tragic bass at work below his words. When we look for the hidden figure in this careful sketch of Nick's fishing trip we find Hemingway himself threaded through field and stream: it is Hemingway's own being which Nick refuses to enter in the tragic shadows and deep water of the swamp. Hemingway, right now as he's writing, does not want to go in there—or he would. Why does he fear the darkness? Well, he doesn't trust himself not to fall apart. We know he's sportsman enough not to drown by accident. He really is crafty enough to go in there. He simply fears the darkness on the underside of things, a possible mental fungus if he disturbs his gathering health with dry fingers, or tries to remove the mental hook from his jaw. Like the grasshoppers, he will be green again in a year's time.

Since it's my job, let me point out that the phrase "He felt a reaction against deep wading . . ." is weak psychology jargon, out of tone with the style, and more strongly might read: "A thought shook him against deep wading . . ."

Henry Thoreau gives us a night scene on a river in *A Week on the Concord and Merrimack Rivers,* an early book he wrote before *Walden:*

The Scene-shifter saw fit here to close the drama of this day without regard to any unities which we mortals prize. Whether it might have proved tragedy, or comedy, or tragicomedy, or pastoral, we cannot tell. This Sunday ended by the going down of the sun, leaving us still on the waves. But they who are on the water enjoy a longer and brighter twilight than they who are on the land, for here the water, as well as the atmosphere, absorbs and reflects the light, and some of the day seems to have sunk down into the waves. The light gradually forsook the deep water, as well as the deeper air, and the gloaming came to the fishes as well as to us, and more dim and gloomy to them, whose day is a perpetual twilight, though sufficiently bright for their weak and watery eyes. Vespers had already rung in many a dim and watery chapel down below, where the shadows of the weeds were extended in length over the sandy floor. The vespertinal pout had already begun to flit on leathern fin, and the finny gossips withdrew from the fluvial street to creeks and coves, and other private haunts, excepting a few of stronger fin, which anchored in the stream, stemming the tide even in their dreams. Meanwhile, like a dark evening cloud, we were wafted over the cope of their sky, deepening the shadows on their deluged fields.

—*A Week on the Concord and Merrimack Rivers* (1847), Henry Thoreau

I'd meant to go on for two more paragraphs, as Thoreau and his friend pitch camp and fall asleep, but I can't put you through it. I can't even type it. Thoreau still writes here in the tired literary humors of his day, which he outgrew by *Walden*. And there's much to learn from failure like this. Why does Henry need to overwrite? Because he has a great urge to write and not much to say, although the middle part stands up well and catches shades of light skillfully. The trouble is that the good part is wrapped in piffle and cowflop.

The first two sentences turn on an error of logic which his jokes don't lighten. He says that dramatic unity fails to happen when he can't tell whether the day ended tragically, comically, tragi-comically, or as pastoral. Then he turns from whatever it is he's left hanging there and states flatly that the day ended with the going down of the sun. I'd say dramatic unity fails because he has no drama, which is why he can't tell how the day ended. The real drama of the paragraph takes place in water. Let me rewrite and try to frame the best parts of this paragraph so they stand out:

God closed Sunday without drama. It ended with the sun going down, leaving us still on the river. But voyagers by water enjoy a longer and brighter twilight than men on land. The water and air absorb and reflect light until some of the day seems to have sunk down into the waves. Bit by bit, light drains from the deep water and the land, and twilight falls on fish and man, but more gloomily on the fishes. Their day is endless twilight, though bright enough for their weak eyes. Weed shadows flowed over the sandy floor. The fish pouted, catching bugs, then fled to creeks and coves, or to other private haunts. A few stronger fish anchored in the stream and stemmed the tide, dreaming. We floated above them on the roof of their sky, our boat a dark evening cloud deepening the shadows of weeds.

Okay, beat me, beat me! But *this* is the way I read things. I depiffle, whether it's Thoreau or God or the *New York Times Book Review.* Now here's Thoreau without flapdoodle:

I was witness to events of a less peaceful character. One day when I went out to my wood-pile, or rather my pile of stumps, I observed two large ants, the one red, the other much larger, nearly half an inch long, and black, fiercely contending with one another. Having once got hold they never let go, but struggled and wrestled and rolled on the chips incessantly. Looking farther, I was surprised to find that the chips were covered with such combatants, that it was not a *duellum,* but a *bellum,* a war between two races of ants, the red always pitted against the black, and frequently two red ones to one black. The legions of these Myrmidons covered all the hills and vales in my wood-yard, and the ground was already strewn with the dead and dying, both red and black. It was the only battle which I have ever witnessed, the only battle-field I ever trod while the battle was raging; internecine war; the red republicans on the one hand,

and the black imperialists on the other. On every side they were engaged in deadly combat, yet without any noise that I could hear, and human soldiers never fought so resolutely. I watched a couple that were fast locked in each other's embraces, in a little sunny valley amid the chips, now at noonday prepared to fight till the sun went down, or life went out. The smaller red champion had fastened himself like a vice to his adversary's front, and through all the tumblings on that field never for an instant ceased to gnaw at one of his feelers near the root, having already caused the other to go by the board; while the stronger black one dashed him from side to side, and, as I saw on looking nearer, had already divested him of several of his members. They fought with more pertinacity than bull-dogs. Neither manifested the least disposition to retreat. It was evident that their battle-cry was Conquer or die. In the mean while there came along a single red ant on the hillside of this valley, evidently full of excitement, who either had despatched his foe, or had not yet taken part in the battle; probably the latter, for he had lost none of his limbs; whose mother had charged him to return with his shield or upon it. Or perchance he was some Achilles, who had nourished his wrath apart, and had now come to avenge or rescue his Patroclus. He saw this unequal combat from afar,—for the blacks were nearly twice the size of the red,—he drew near with rapid pace till he stood on his guard within half an inch of the combatants; then, watching his opportunity, he sprang upon the black warrior, and commenced his operations near the root of his right fore-leg, leaving the foe to select among his own members; and so there were three united for life, as if a new kind of attraction had been invented which put all other locks and cements to shame. I should not have wondered by this time to find that they had their respective musical bands stationed on some eminent chip, and playing their national airs the while, to excite the slow and cheer the dying combatants. I was myself excited somewhat even as if they had been men. The more you think of it, the less the difference. . . . [The battle goes on for two more pages.]

—*Walden* (1854), Henry Thoreau

Gone are the Scene-shifter, the unities we mortals prize, the vespertinal pout, finny gossips, bloated phrasings such as "they who are on the water" for voyagers and "they who are on the land" for men on land. One reason for this: Thoreau revised *Walden* eight times, sweating the style down to real matter. He couldn't get one of his earlier versions published, lucky guy, and so rewhittled himself a masterpiece instead.

Not that the battle of the ants hasn't flaws. I'd like "not a duel but a war" for "not a *duellum,* but a *bellum,*" "killers" for "Myrmidons," "insect slaughtering insect" for "internecine war," "fast locked" for "fast locked in each other's embraces" (a cut which sings; and if they are fast locked, there's only one embrace), "gnaw at the root of a feeler" for "gnaw at one of his feelers near the root," "cut off many members" for "divested him of several of his members," "more savagery" for "more pertinacity," "neither would quit" for "neither manifested the least disposition to retreat," "clear" for "evident," "killed" for "despatched," and so on. Would all these prickings of overblown words improve Thoreau? For me, yes! The battle of the ants stands out in *Walden* for its action, not its richness. Richer action with less self-amusement would boost this passage. I'm uplifted by Thoreau's stylistic improvement, through intense self-editing, from *Week* to *Walden.* It's not just that one passage above is inspired and the other tired. It's word choice, not content, that boosts his intensity and gives life. After an electrical eighth revision brings down bolts from heaven, Henry cries through the rain on his pond, "It's alive! It's alive!"

Another example of a boost in vividness comes from Orson Welles's script for *The Magnificent Ambersons*. Every word of the climactic scene is taken from Booth Tarkington's novel (1918). George Amberson Minafer, an unbearably bumptious Midwestern aristocrat whose family has gone bust, finds himself stripped of place and money. Welles condenses several pages about this turning point in George's life into two paragraphs of voice-over storytelling in the novel's own words. I should add that in this film Welles's mellow voice, at its absolute ripest, takes on a lush joy at the elegiac images on screen and in this scene softens to a God-like pity beyond irony. During his reading on the sound track we watch George walk home through his once small Indiana town while image melts into image of dingy housefronts and mansions now turned into Elks Clubs and funeral homes:

WELLES *(voice-over)*: George Amberson Minafer walked homeward slowly through what seemed to be the strange streets of a strange city. For the town was growing, changing. It was heaving up in the middle, incredibly. It was spreading incredibly. It had heaved and spread, it befouled itself and darkened its sky. This was the last walk home he was ever to take on National Avenue to Amberson Addition, to the big old house at the foot of Amberson Boulevard. Tomorrow they were to move out. Tomorrow everything would be gone.

Something had happened, a thing which years ago had been the eagerest hope of many, many good citizens of the town. And now it came at last. George Amberson Minafer had got his comeuppance. He had got it three times filled and running over. But those who had so longed for it were not there to see it. They never knew. Those who were still living had forgotten all about it, and all about him.

GEORGE (*kneeling in darkness, arms outstretched and clutching at the covers of a shadowy bed*): Mother, forgive me! *God,* forgive me!

SLOW DISSOLVE TO: Shot of the Amberson Mansion—massive as the old house is, it manages to look gaunt: its windows stare with the skull emptiness of all windows in empty houses that are to be lived in no more.

—*The Magnificent Ambersons* (film; 1942), Orson Welles/
   Booth Tarkington

Immensely faithful to Tarkington, Welles's script states all his shot setups in the novel's words. In the shooting script the walk home has what would be five or six minutes of shots and dialogue, straight from the novel, but in the finished film Welles cuts the walk and George's prayer to a briefer playing time. "Finished film" should be in quotes: RKO butchered forty-eight minutes of Welles's director's cut—and the nitrate outtakes are now dust.

What makes this passage so moving? Simplicity, and our sense that it's really about something—and not about the movie son of a Hollywood movie family. The first paragraph shows George estranged by his hometown as it spreads and heaves and darkens the sky and befouls itself, as happens in the novel with the coming of the automobile. City streets are paved for cars and trucks, factories mushroom and soak homes with soot from coal and coke. The automobile causes property values to shift and Amberson Mansion becomes a massive skull. "Tomorrow they were to move out. Tomorrow everything would be gone."

Welles's voice-over repeats Tarkington's "heaved" and "heaving" because—just as the tragic swamp is Nick Adams's and Hemingway's own deeper nature—the eruption of the streets and falling filth is George's repressed lower nature bursting his veneer of snobbery. The ripe, psalm-like voice hovers on the images and goes from cityscape to George's crisis, which leaves him praying at his dead mother's bed as Welles builds from simple phrases to a climactic biblical image, the bitter cup of George's comeuppance, the great unblinding on which the novel turns: "And now it came at last. George Amberson Minafer had got his comeuppance. He had got it three times filled [pause] and running over."

The most famous night scene near water in modern times is Nick Carraway's description of his neighbor's parties in "the great wet barnyard of Long Island Sound":

There was music from my neighbor's house through the summer nights. In his blue gardens men and girls came and went like moths among the whisperings and the champagne and the stars. . . .

. . . The last swimmers have come in from the beach now and are dressing upstairs; the cars from New York are parked five deep at the drive, and already the halls and salons and verandas are gaudy with primary colors and hair shorn in strange new ways and shawls beyond the dreams of Castile. The bar is in full swing and floating rounds of cocktails permeate the garden outside until the air is alive with chatter and laughter and casual innuendo and introductions forgotten on the spot and enthusiastic meetings between women who never knew each other's names.

The lights grow brighter as the earth lurches away from the sun and now the orchestra is playing yellow cocktail music and the opera of voices pitches a key higher. Laughter is easier, minute by minute, spilled with prodigality, tipped out at a cheerful word. The groups change more swiftly, swell with new arrivals, dissolve and form in the same breath—already there are wanderers, confident girls who weave here and there among the stouter and more stable, become for a sharp, joyous moment the center of a group and then excited with triumph glide on through the sea-change of faces and voices and color under the constantly changing light.

—*The Great Gatsby* (1925), F. Scott Fitzgerald

Fitzgerald's magic springs in part from statements stripped as naked of commas and hyphens as good sense allows—even though Nick is in the bond business and boning up on banking and credit and investment securities and would overly Latinize his English like any investment analyst faced with a pen. The mind takes in this scene fluidly as a camera lens. I much abridge, but throughout it Fitzgerald washes the scene with blue gardens and primary colors, yellow, orange, lemon, "enough colored lights to make a Christmas tree," brass, "salons and verandas gaudy with primary colors," even yellow cocktail music, and rounds out this inventory with "voices and color under the constantly changing light." Aside from a dark gold turkey, no shade is subtle.

The wary reader now asks, Well, Don, what about "permeate"? Leave it. ". . . floating rounds of cocktails pass through the garden" is fine, and "floating rounds of cocktails permeate the garden" just as fine. FEAR NO LATIN!—not if it doesn't drain life. But it usually makes me sneeze and my ears ring.

I like the birdwhistle and deep bass of Anglo-Saxon, and to squat down and break up smelly life-giving manure with my fingers and rub damp, fresh loam over my face and trade grips with a living tongue. Latin's for poor blowflies in the priestcrafts and subsciences squeezing eggs onto the eyes of the dead. Nothing's more to the point than Anglo-Saxon; it shows up mumbo jumbo, double-talk, and rot in the sentence tissue. But I rant, yes I rant, and will be whipped for it. What's worse, I may be wrong. Surely there is some priest or surgeon trained in Latin who can make that stone-dead tongue sing like Anglo-Saxon. . . .

In the period of which we speak [eighteenth-century France], there reigned in the cities a stench barely conceivable to us modern men and women. The streets stank of manure, the courtyards of urine, the stairwells stank of moldering wood and rat droppings, the kitchens of spoiled cabbage and mutton fat; the unaired parlors stank of stale dust, the bedrooms of greasy sheets, damp featherbeds, and the pungently sweet aroma of chamber pots. The stench of sulfur rose from the chimneys, the stench of caustic lyes from the tanneries, and from the slaughterhouses came the stench of congealed blood. People stank of sweat and unwashed clothes; from their mouths came the stench of rotting teeth, from their bellies that of onions, and from their bodies, if they were no longer very young, came the stench of rancid cheese and sour milk and tumorous disease. The rivers stank, the marketplaces stank, the churches stank, it stank beneath the bridges and in the palaces. The peasant stank as did the priest, the apprentice as did his master's wife, the whole of the aristocracy stank, even the king himself stank, stank like a rank lion, and the queen like an old goat, summer and winter. For in the eighteenth century there was nothing to hinder bacteria busy at decomposition, and so there was no human activity, either constructive or destructive, no manifestation of germinating or decaying life that was not accompanied by stench.

—*Perfume: The Story of a Murderer* (1986), Patrick Suskind, translated from the German by John E. Woods

Now there's plenty of good rich Latin. The smells lift right off the page. But, aha, on second sniff, aside from the last sentence, it's all in the heady loveliness of Anglo-Saxon and richly smoked Middle English. And laid on like Limburger with onions, two ales on the side, please, would you wipe the table? I see a sign on the throne: NO PISSING ON THE PALACE FLOOR!

In this novel, Grenouille, a perfumer's monstrous apprentice and a genius of the nose, knows infinitely more about scents than his master, Baldini, although his training in the art and trade of powders and perfumery goes on for many ripely fragrant and richly dusted pages. Reading Suskind is like falling dead drunk in a distillery amid huge casks of sour mash. I must say, the translation shines, all Latin fits the time and place, and I clap Mr. Woods's back for his good work and award him the Medal of the Nose for his Anglo-Saxon.

And here is some blood-lifting Latin from retired surgeon Richard Selzer, who in his memoirs says farewell to the inner organs he fondled for so many years:

> One enters the body in surgery as in love. . . . Do not fear the yellow meadows of fat, the red that sweats and trickles where you step. . . . Now rest a bit upon the peritoneum. All at once, the gleaming membrane parts, and you are in. . . . Touch the great artery, feel it bound like a deer in the might of its lightness and know the thunderless boil of the blood. Lean for a moment against this bone. It is the only memento you will leave to the earth. Its tacitness is everlasting. Press your ear against this body the way a child holds a seashell and hears faintly the half-remembered, longed for sea. . . . In the canals, cilia paddle quiet as an Iroquois canoe. Somewhere nearby a white whip slide of tendon bows across a joint. Now there *is* sound, small splashings, tunneled currents of air. Slow, gaseous bubbles ascend through dark, unlit lakes. Across the diaphragm and into the chest: Here at least it is all noise, the whisper of the lung, the *lub dup, lub dup* of the garrulous heart. Such a primitive place. One expects to find drawings of buffalo on the walls. The sense of trespassing is heightened by the world's light illuminating the organs, their secret colors revealed, maroon and salmon and yellow. An arc of the liver shines high on the right like a dark sun. It laps over the pink sweep of the stomach,

from whose lower border the gauzy omentum is draped and through whose veil one sees like sinuous, slow as just-fed snakes, the indolent coils of the intestine.

—*Down from Troy: A Doctor Comes of Age*
(1992), Richard Selzer

Despite a thoughtful pace and steady cut at each word, Selzer handles this aria with great bravura and even works toward a rising action that delivers an apt likeness of the indolent coils of the intestines to sinuous, slow as just-fed snakes. I've never seen that odd last bit of grammar before—but like it here.

How does he pull off this triumph? First he disarms us by inviting us into his love affair. That's always helpful. After all, he's just an exile returning at last to his heart (the patient's, of course). *Is* he an exile? Well, he's been away writing! Now he's come home, bringing you along. Turn sideways and slip into this secret cleft with him. Delicately, he warns about blood underfoot on the yellow meadows of fat. But don't fear it, dear heart, it's just a red sweat.

Once we surrender to his voice, we're ready for the tour. I've abridged it but he tells about the awful quiet of ruins and rainbows within and draws us into deep literary puddles where he pulls out one fresh-washed likeness after another. "Touch the great artery, feel it bound like a deer in the might of its lightness and know the thunderless boil of the blood." Wow. This bone, it's all you ever leave to the earth. Hm. Here you can hear the sea in the seashell of childhood. Suddenly we're down among the microscopic, the paddling cilia, but jump right out again, somewhere near a white tendon bowed onto a

71

joint. I thought we were in the chest, frankly, not near any joint. The muddle builds with "Across the diaphragm and into the chest." Hell, I'd already cranked up the sternum. Where've we been all this time? Whispering lung, talkative heart. "Such a primitive place." Really? What's so primitive? It hasn't changed since early man, Doctor. "One expects to find drawings of buffalo on the walls." Aha, you're just joking. Yes, he's disarmed us still again, because now he's going in for the kill. Here comes the release of the paragraph's tensions, the fireworks: ". . . the world's light illuminating the organs [actually, not the world's light but fluorescence], their secret colors revealed, maroon and salmon and yellow." For that, which I'll remember all my life, I'll forgive Selzer any sin. "An arc of the liver shines high on the right like a dark sun." Damn! I thought this was heart surgery and we're down at the liver. Or going after an appendix—some love affair this is. "It laps over the pink sweep of the stomach, from whose lower border the gauzy omentum is draped. . . ." This is well said. The gauzy omentum is a fatty skin draped under the stomach, and Selzer draws it with the liver lapped "over the pink sweep of the stomach," the omentum draped and gauzy, a veil through which we can see the sinuous indolence of just-fed snakes, the intestines.

This may be no desert island guide to surgery, but it sure as hell is great illustration. The colors, the great artery bounding like a deer, the seashell silence of the inner organs, slow gaseous bubbles from unlit lakes. He has stripped his mistress for us and is pointing out the choice parts. But, she's so beautiful and he's such a poet, he doesn't know where to begin. He starts with her yellow meadows of fat—a great idea!

Let's switch from surgery to radiology. In this passage, young

Hans Castorp, Thomas Mann's hero in *The Magic Mountain,* has fallen in love with Frau Chauchat, a fellow tuberculosis patient at a hospital high in the Swiss Alps. Earlier, invited into the private quarters of Hofrat Behrens, the hospital director, he'd been shown a painting of Frau Chauchat done by Dr. Behrens. Later Dr. Behrens gives Hans a glass-plate X-ray negative, one he used in painting Frau Chauchat practically "subcutaneously."

It was a small negative. Held in the same plane with the ground, it was black and opaque; but lifted against the light, it revealed matter for a humanistic eye: the transparent reproduction of the human form, the bony framework of the ribs, the outline of the heart, the arch of the diaphragm, the bellows that were the lungs; together with the shoulder and upper-arm bones, all shrouded in a dim and vaporous envelope of flesh—that flesh which once, in Carnival week, Hans Castorp had so madly tasted. What wonder that his unstable heart stood still or wildly throbbed when he gazed at it. . . .

—*The Magic Mountain* (1924), Thomas Mann,
translated from the German by H. T. Lowe-Porter

Hans carries the glass plate with him everywhere and at times, when alone, takes it out to study his beloved's inner organs—much like Dr. Selzer! As I said, we've switched from surgery to radiology and this must be the first X-ray portrait of a heroine ever done. I see Mann's rolling eye and lip-licking catsmile as he thinks of this device, which weds the utmost up-to-date medical technology with the inner being of Frau Chauchat. See her take shape in the blue smoke of his morning cigar.

And how sexy! You can almost put your hand inside her birth-day suit. Never been done before. Will I knock 'em dead with this! My God, this throbbing, I can't breathe. Thomas, isn't this almost criminal? Mmm!

The turning point in Mann's *Death in Venice* comes at novel's end when the weary middle-aged writer Aschenbach, who is resting his nerves in Venice, finds himself electrified and besot-ted by an angelic male adolescent, sits in a barber's chair and allows his tired old head to be remade for the boy beauty. At the same time he has been revamping himself, brightening his dress with smart ties, handkerchiefs, jewelry and perfume. When he sits in the barber chair, he sighs, "Grey." The alert, sympathetic barber sells him on restoring his hair "to your nat-ural color," then dyes it as "black as in the days of his youth" and waves it with tongs.

"Now if we were just to freshen up the skin a little," he said.

And with that he went on from one thing to another, his enthusiasm waxing with each new idea. Aschenbach sat there comfortably; he was incapable of objecting to the pro-cess—rather as it went forward it roused his hopes. He watched it in the mirror and saw his eyebrows grow more even and arching, the eyes gain in size and brilliance, by dint of a little application below the lids. A delicate carmine glowed in his cheeks where the skin had been so brown and leathery. The dry, anemic lips grew full, they turned the color of ripe strawberries, the lines round eyes and mouth were treated with a facial cream and gave place to youthful bloom. It was a young man who looked back at him from the glass—Aschenbach's heart leaped at the sight. The artist in cosmetic at last professed himself satisfied; after the manner of such people, he thanked his client profusely for what he had done himself. "The merest trifle, the merest, signore," he said as he added the final touches. "Now the signore can fall in love as soon as he likes." Aschenbach went off as in a dream, dazed between joy and fear, in his red necktie and broad straw hat with its gay striped band.

—*Death in Venice* (1912), Thomas Mann,
translated from the German by H. T. Lowe-Porter

The reader's feelings in this passage weigh not only his or her investment in Aschenbach but also one's own sweet daydream about recovering youth. This is one of the most magnetic moments in all of Mann. The reader finds himself or herself sucked body and soul into Aschenbach's sick hopes and sitting in the barber chair for embalming. Aschenbach gives up utterly and melts into a sappiness unto death.

Throughout the story he meets the figure of Death in many guises, a knotting of Aschenbach into his fate that wins Mann many puffs on his cigar as each new figure shows up. Giving oneself strokes for inventiveness builds your spirit—don't hold back! A writer's happiness—often at its height during the worst days of his life—goes straight into the page and sparks the ideal reader to award prizes. What sped Mann through his twelve-hundred-page *Joseph and His Brothers* or *The Magic Mountain*'s nine hundred pages? Joy! Telling himself, Boy, I write good—his eyes, cracks in a crusty loaf. Mann tells us in *A Sketch of My Life* (1930) about writing *Death in Venice*: ". . . as I worked on this story—as always it was a long-drawn-out job—I had at moments the clearest feelings of transcendence, a sovereign

75

sense of being borne up such as I had never before experienced."
So, give strokes, allow in the divine wind—the more open you
keep yourself, the more likely will come that first agreeable
ringing on the chimes within, a happy battering which awakes
without warning, never by act of will.

Even with transcendence, Mann came to dislike the forced
symbolism in Aschenbach's last vision of his beloved Tadzio as
the "pale and lovely Summoner": Aschenbach at last fully meets
Tadzio's "twilit grey eyes" as the boy stands gazing at him in
low water on the Lido beach, then points outward "into an immensity of richest expectation"—and Aschenbach fades away
into a Mahlerian night (Mann modeled him on himself and
Mahler, whom he thought the one undeniably great man he'd
ever met). Mann even told his brother Heinrich the story was
"not good enough" and "full of half-baked ideas and falsehoods"
(see *The Brothers Mann* by Nigel Hamilton).

Mann sets up Aschenbach's visit to the fountain of false
youth by exciting him, giving him agonies, tarting him up
laughably with jewels and sprays, then shriveling him with
self-disgust. The oily barber finds no resistance from the great
writer under his fingers. Lo, gray turns black, eyeliner gives the
eyes bigness and brilliance, the brown and leathery cheeks are
rouged, the lips made into ripe strawberries, the crow's-feet
creamed and brought to youthful bloom. A young man looks
back at Aschenbach from the glass—his heart leaps at the
sight. He's been suckered by a con man in cosmetics and loves
it. Morally dead, he goes off "as in a dream, dazed between joy
and fear, in his red neck-tie and broad straw hat with its gay
striped band." When the plague quickly carries off his body—
a few, foolishly eaten overripe strawberries from a sultry market
stall do the infecting—that's just Mann carting off the rubbish.

From sultry Venice in the grip of plague, we leap to sultry Los Angeles in the grip of Joan Didion:

There is something uneasy in the Los Angeles air this afternoon, some unnatural stillness, some tension. What it means is that tonight a Santa Ana will begin to blow, a hot wind from the northeast whining down through the Cajon and San Gorgonio passes, blowing up sandstorms out along Route 66, drying the hills and the nerves to the flash point. For a few days now we will see smoke back in the canyons, and hear sirens in the night. I have neither heard nor read that a Santa Ana is due, but I know it, and almost everyone I have seen today knows it too. We know it because we feel it. The baby frets. The maid sulks. I rekindle a waning argument with the telephone company, then cut my losses and lie down, given over to whatever it is in the air. To live with the Santa Ana is to accept, consciously or unconsciously, a deeply mechanistic view of human behavior. I recall being told, when I first moved to Los Angeles and was living on an isolated beach, that the Indians would throw themselves into the sea when the bad wind blew. I could see why. The Pacific turned ominously glossy during a Santa Ana period, and one woke in the night troubled not only by the peacocks screaming in the olive trees but by the eerie absence of surf. The heat was surreal. The sky had a yellow cast, the kind of light sometimes called "earthquake weather." My only neighbor would not come out of her house for days. . . .

—"Los Angeles Notebook" (1965–1967),
Slouching Towards Bethlehem (1978), Joan Didion

And the neighbor would not light her lights at night, and her husband roamed about with a machete, telling Didion about a trespasser he'd heard, then a rattlesnake. Then she quotes Raymond Chandler, who once wrote about the Santa Ana: ". . . every booze party ends in a fight. Meek little wives feel the edge of the carving knife and study their husbands' necks. Anything can happen." It's that kind of wind. (I wish Chandler had said "thumb," not "feel.")

Didion goes on to tell of like evil winds in Austria, Switzerland, Israel, France and the Mediterranean. After listing possible causes for the big zap in these winds, she tells that an Israeli physicist found in Israel's bad wind an unusually high ratio of positive to negative ions. Others suggest solar disturbances. But she goes with an excess of positive ions and the mechanistic idea that these make people unhappy in the catastrophic and apocalyptic Los Angeles weather and bring on violence and unpredictability. That wind drives us to the edge.

A masterful opening leads bit by bit downhill until by this piece's end Didion sits amid drunks in a piano bar, doing nothing. "Why not," she says—not even making a question of it.

She leads with her best stuff, shows her own flakiness, unloads a paragraph of research, then has no place to go. So she falls back on flakiness, listens to radio talk drivel, drives to Ralph's Market in her old bikini bathing suit (is she swacked? we wonder), pointlessly goes to a party that may or may not tell us something about the Santa Ana, and winds up in a bar.

The odd part of the story is that the start is so tight and full of tension. She shows us how to write a high-quality bit of confessional journalism. By midarticle she's so loose that her deeply mechanistic view of human behavior has no more force than a supermarket tabloid. A great article dribbles away. But that's part of her argument and makes plain the effects of a wind overcharged with positive ions. She entertains throughout, but as energy drains, so does the piece. I see her crawl to the corner mailbox to mail it, happy to get it out of the house.

Here's a short description from her novel *Play It As It Lays:*

> In January there were poinsettias in front of all the bungalows between Melrose and Sunset, and the rain set in, and Maria wore not sandals but real shoes and a Shetland sweater she had bought in New York the year she was nineteen. For days during the rain she did not speak out loud or read a newspaper. She could not read newspapers because certain stories leapt at her from the page: the four-year-olds in the abandoned refrigerator, the tea party with Purex, the infant in the driveway, rattlesnake in the playpen, the peril, unspeakable peril, in the everyday. She grew faint as the processions swept before her, the children alive when last scolded, dead when next seen, the children in the locked car burning, the little faces, helpless screams. The mothers were always reported to be under sedation. In the whole world there was not as much sedation as there was instantaneous peril. Maria ate frozen enchiladas, looked at television for word of the world, thought of herself as under sedation and did not leave the apartment on Fountain Avenue.

> —*Play It As It Lays* (1970), Joan Didion

Didion's effect in her early fiction and journalism is one of deadpan parody pulled off as clinically black moods. She carries it off brilliantly, if falling short of the great daddy of such writing, August Strindberg, whose torment in *Inferno* (1897) becomes positively occult, until the walls discharge bolts into him. But Strindberg is first a dramatist, even in this memoir, which is drawn from a recent diary with his pains still fresh on the page, and he sketches his own nuttiness so intensely that one senses self-parody. Didion's deadpan satire is so deadpan that readers likely take her stand-ins for the real woman, not artistic creations. I think Didion must laugh a lot privately as she drives pains into her other selves—although on a recent TV talk show hosted by Charlie Rose, she gasped or grimaced more than laughed, as if—overtaken by art—she'd grown into her own monster but now is shedding that image for one of a grown-up speaking for others. In her searing *Salvador* (1982), she abandons self-parody and drives pains into *us*. But I sound like a *Vanity Fair* shrinkpiece on celebrityhood.

What's worse, I will go on sounding like a magazine gossip, because now I want to quote a memoir that's all tattle. I loved this book. It moved me to High Reviewerese when I reviewed it: "That cloudless rarity, a book that you hope will never end."

Carol Matthau's *Among the Porcupines* tells of life with her two best friends, millionairess Gloria Vanderbilt and Oona O'Neill, daughter of Eugene O'Neill and wife of Charlie Chaplin; of Matthau's marriages to writer William Saroyan (twice!) and actor Walter Matthau; and of her lifelong friendship with Truman Capote. I find something at once concrete and cloud-borne in Carol's voice that binds me to the sheer openness of her feelings—and the honesty of her lies. She figures into Capote's bloodletting on high society, the novel *Answered Prayers*. Here she shows her hand at portraiture of husband Walter, a man not given to bestowing affection loosely:

Dear Oona,

Just so you will know: Walter is a very selfish man who happened to get the greatest housekeeper of all time because I was the very best, until a few years ago when I got sick and now I am only slightly less than my best. I'm having gardener trouble. Walter doesn't want to know, he doesn't want to hear, he does not have time to deal with it in any way because he and his bookie are tremendously busy most of the day and night. And I get fucking mad.

We have a dead tree in our garden and we have spent thousands and thousands of dollars trying to keep it alive. I think it's a worthwhile thing to do. It's just that I'd like a little encouragement from him.

"Aren't you perfect? You are keeping a dead tree alive."

Something like that would do, but simply isn't forthcoming. . . .

. . . What I am saying is that he has my guts, my heart, my soul. He's taken all of me and hasn't the slightest notion of what is involved here. He doesn't want to hear about the houses, he doesn't want to know about them, he never says that anything is nice, and always says when something is wrong. . . .

—*Among the Porcupines* (1992), Carol Matthau

Matthau's skillful portrait of a laughing, selfish sonofabitch shows love despite Walter's day-and-night gambling and readiness to bet the ground away from under her feet—and her royalties too. She fights back by whiting out the last zero on the price tags of her nighties, which I call the honesty of her lies.

Before we look into her style—which is her own but stems from such ditzy high-society ladies of thirties film farce as Carole Lombard's wacky rich girl in *My Man Godfrey* or Billie Burke's beautifully gowned, deliciously confused Mrs. Cosmo Topper who joins fingers at her pelvis and manfully stands up to Cosmo's chaos—let's read Matthau's note on the death of Charlie Chaplin. She tells of the Christmas Day that Charlie died and of Oona going into deep mourning. She remembers that she and Oona once read an uplifting passage from Willa Cather's *Lucy Gayheart* together, so she tears that passage out of her first edition (given to her by Oona) and mails it to her. The passage is about a young widow lifted out of mourning by thoughts of her old hometown sweetheart. She takes to dressing up and dreaming about him, but when she actually runs across him one day the meeting is sad. That night she stands looking out the window in her room and sees snow falling—white, lacy snow with blue lights, quite magical. She opens the window and for a long time watches snow fall, then puts one hand out, almost to her elbow, then the other.

> And then she put her face out and let the snow fall on it, and it made her face feel wonderful. She looked up above the trees to the sky, which was filled with beautiful white snow, swirling, gently falling on leaves, trees, ground, rooftops. And she loved watching it. And suddenly she knew something. That old sweetheart is life itself.

In her description of Walter and her gardening, Matthau comes on as a screwball comedienne whose specialty is deadpan marital agony. Her first two marriages, to Saroyan, train her for the miseries of a gambler's wife. Life with Walter is a masterpiece of pain and smiles. I find her voice well judged and her word choice flawless throughout, without a false syllable to mar the makeup she applies to the deep holes of crazy Bill's and laughing Walter's husbandly fang wounds on her neck.

With Chaplin's death in mind, and Oona's later death by alcohol, she strives for upbeat sadness. The snowfall letter avoids overrichness, and its simple words allow magic to enter slowly into the release as Oona/Lucy leans out into the flakes. She keeps light and songful, despite the two deaths pooled at her ankles as she writes. This is the hallmark of her half-smiling-through-agonies style, a withholding that lets us feel the unsaid, the full chill of what she pays to stay warm amid the bristles of porcupines. Even as perfect pitch keeps her naughty words from offending, only this lightness, this resistance to violating her tone, gives deep force to her capping line, which would be a weak thought if undermined ahead by tragic diction: "That old sweetheart is life itself."

Very moving.

Admirable in a much different, superbly overrich way is Capote's description of a bottle of champagne at Manhattan's La Côte Basque, the chic restaurant in which he bloodies the social swans who have taken him in, with swipes at Carol Marcus Saroyan Saroyan Matthau, Oona O'Neill Chaplin, Gloria Vanderbilt de Cicco Stokowski Lumet Cooper, Jacqueline Bouvier Kennedy, her sister Lee Bouvier Radziwill, Barbara Cushing (Babe) Paley, the former Nancy Gross then Slim Hawks Hayward Keith, and Truman's other long-named best buddies in high society. He accompanies Lady Ina Coolbirth to the restaurant, and is given the perfect table by the distrait M. Soulé, a man "pink and glazed as a marzipan pig."

"Lady Coolbirth . . ." he muttered, his perfectionist eyes spinning about in search of cankered roses and awkward waiters. "Lady Coolbirth . . . umn . . . very nice . . . umn . . . and Lord Coolbirth? . . . umn . . . today we have on the wagon a very nice saddle of lamb . . ."

She consulted me, a glance, and said: "I think not anything off the wagon. It arrives too quickly. Let's have something that takes forever. So that we can get drunk and disorderly. Say a soufflé Furstenberg. Could you do that, Monsieur Soulé?"

He tutted his tongue—on two counts: he disapproves of customers dulling their taste buds with alcohol, and also: "Furstenberg is a great nuisance. An uproar."

Delicious, though: a froth of cheese and spinach into which an assortment of poached eggs has been sunk strategically, so that, when struck by your fork, the soufflé is moistened with golden rivers of egg yolk.

"An uproar," said Ina, "is exactly what I want," and the proprietor, touching his sweat-littered forehead with a bit of handkerchief, acquiesced.

Then she decided against cocktails, saying: "Why not have a proper reunion?" From the wine steward she ordered a bottle of Roederer's Cristal. Even for those who dislike champagne, myself among them, there are two champagnes one can't refuse: Dom Pérignon and the even superior Cristal, which is bottled in a natural-colored glass that displays its pale blaze, a chilled fire of such prickly dryness that, swallowed, seems not to have been swallowed at all, but instead to have turned to vapors on the tongue and burned there to one damp sweet ash.

—"La Côte Basque, 1965," *Answered Prayers*
(1986), Truman Capote

Casting aside the scandal this piece made, I none the less read it with mixed feelings. This chapter, for me, is Capote's single most brilliant stretch of words. It's disgusting, funny, harms living people, and heaps up untruths that destroy much of my pleasure in the rest. Nonetheless, time may well find in this chapter's glitter the brightest pages on Capote's shelf. Reviewers savaged the book's tastelessness. Okay, it's gross, but I think it's his best. Why don't I think *In Cold Blood* his best?—a quite chilling work when it first saw ink in 1965 as a seriously researched and well-wrought *New Yorker* serial. Well, after the lies littering *Answered Prayers* I wonder about that earlier research, even though Capote is not a figure in *In Cold Blood* and in no obvious way undermines his research with ego. But more importantly, when I take down *In Cold Blood*—or *any* of his other works—I'm not tempted to read much of them. *Answered Prayers* hooks me for pages. That counts.

The bottle of Roederer Cristal is important to his story: it's the DRINK ME that allows Alice into Wonderland, Alice being Lady Coolbirth's table companion, Capote as P. B. Jones. Capote later claimed he was Lady Coolbirth as well. True, all authors are their fictional characters. But the legendary allure of this champagne unlocks Lady Coolbirth's tongue and she tells Jones things best left untold. Is Capote really talking to himself and blaming morally deplorable lies about his friends on champagne?

He sets up the champagne by first spreading before us the uproar and nuisance of soufflé Furstenberg with its froth of cheese and spinach, moistened with golden rivers of egg yolk. "An uproar is exactly what I want," says Ina/Truman, wanting to dizzy us before going into her act. However, she will never get an "assortment of poached eggs" unless they are dyed or a combo of duck, goose and chicken eggs: poached chicken eggs do not come assorted. They are chicken eggs. Capote's waving charms in our eyes.

Then, the champagne. You can't refuse it, even though P.J. dislikes champagne. Well, if we're going to dish this dirt, let's get on with it, yipes. A pale blaze in "natural-colored glass" (isn't natural glass colorless?), "a chilled fire of such prickly dryness that, swallowed, seems not to have been swallowed at all, but instead to have turned to vapors on the tongue and burned there to one damp sweet ash."

With magic potions like that, who can keep quiet? But the truth is, I think from experience, that Roederer's Cristal is a learned taste, like Turkish tobacco, crabmeat, and many odd foods or partly poisonous drinks. Many readers downing a glass of Cristal would find it like swallowing cold ashes, and with an *unsweet* ashy aftertaste. The Cristal is one more con job, attracting belief in the writer's good faith. 'Nuff said.

Capote is never passionate except about words, although *In Cold Blood* has some moving moments in windowpane prose. Here he is pitch-perfect as a countertenor. Later, in John Bunyan, we'll look over some words that bear spiritual passion and really finger the heartstrings. But the passage above is one I admire for word choice and the ear of an angel. A naughty, even nasty, angel, but nevertheless an angel. Capote rises above his flaws here with a style that for me flattens his critics. Real writing wakes the dead writer from his dust and stands him before us. No one can deny that Capote wakes from the dead on every page in *Answered Prayers.* And ten years or twenty from now I'll weigh once more what I think of the fabulous but mean-spirited talent that wrote "La Côte Basque."

So let's turn to Capote's master, the most great-spirited *Van-*

ity Fair writer of them all, and follow this description of his release from deepest gloom toward the end of his last novel:

But it is sometimes just at the moment when we think that everything is lost that the intimation arrives which may save us; one has knocked at all the doors which lead nowhere, and then one stumbles without knowing it on the only door through which one can enter—which one might have sought in vain for a hundred years—and it opens of its own accord. Revolving the gloomy thoughts which I have just recorded, I had entered the courtyard of the Guermantes mansion and in my absent-minded state I had failed to see a car which was coming towards me; the chauffeur gave a shout and I just had time to step out of the way, but as I moved sharply backwards I tripped against the uneven paving-stones in front of the coach-house. And at the moment when, recovering my balance, I put my food on a stone which was slightly lower than its neighbor, all my discouragement vanished and in its place was that same happiness which at various epochs of my life had been given to me by the sight of trees which I had thought that I recognized in the course of a drive near Balbec, by the sight of the twin steeples of Martinville, by the flavor of a madeleine dipped in tea, and by all those other sensations of which I have spoken and of which the last works of Vinteuil [a composer] had seemed to me to combine the quintessential character. Just as, at the moment when I tasted the madeleine, all anxiety about the future, all intellectual doubts had disappeared, so now those that a few seconds ago had assailed me on the subject of the reality of my literary gifts, the reality even of literature, were removed as if by magic. I had followed no new train of reasoning, discovered no decisive argument, but the difficulties which had seemed insoluble a moment ago had lost all importance. The happiness which I had just felt was unquestionably the same as that which I had felt when I tasted the madeleine soaked in tea. But if on that occasion I had put off the task of searching for the profounder causes of my emotion, this time I was determined not to resign myself to a failure to understand them. The emotion was the same; the difference, purely material, lay in the images evoked: a profound azure intoxicated my eyes, impressions of coolness, of dazzling light, swirled around me and in my desire to seize them—as afraid to move as I had been on the earlier occasion when I had continued to savor the taste of the madeleine while I tried to draw into my consciousness whatever it was that it recalled to me—I continued, ignoring the evident amusement of the great crowd of chauffeurs, to stagger as I had staggered a few seconds ago, with one foot on the higher paving-stone and the other on the lower. Every time that I merely repeated this physical movement, I achieved nothing; but if I succeeded, forgetting the Guermantes party, in recapturing what I had felt when I first placed my feet on the ground in this way, again the dazzling and indistinct vision fluttered near me, as if to say: "Seize me as I pass if you can, and try to solve the riddle of happiness which I set you." And almost at once I recognized the vision: it was Venice, of which my efforts to describe it and the supposed snapshots taken by my memory had never told me anything, but which the sensation which I had once experienced as I stood upon two uneven stones in the baptistry of St. Mark's had, recurring a moment ago, restored to me complete with all the other sensations linked on that day to the particular sensation, all of which had been waiting in their place—from which with imperious suddenness a chance happening had caused them to emerge—in the series of forgotten days. In the same way the taste of the little madeleine had recalled Combray to me. But why had the images of Combray and of Venice, at these two different moments, given me a joy which was like a certainty and which sufficed, without any other proof, to make death a matter of indifference to me?

—*Time Regained* (1927), translated by Andreas Mayor; from the 1981 Random House three-volume edition of *Remembrance of Things Past* (1913–1927), Marcel Proust

This is a fairly clear translation, though a better one is promised us from Richard Howard, who has been retonguing the seven novels of *Remembrance of Things Past* for several years. The whole, now called *In Search of Lost Time,* apparently will be published all at once—and a glowing June day that'll be!

One must surrender to Proust as to a symphony. And to the translator, trusting that his and Proust's sentence will work out sensibly. I often get lost in the clauses, then find they make sense. Proust writes in something better than a drone but I find myself taking in the words at a steady clip that neither expects nor allows emotional highs and lows, or the sudden throb Carol Matthau gets into "That old sweetheart is life itself." His effects arrive in more of a glowy haze.

What gloom he's in on his train journey from the sanitorium! But you don't have to be a failed writer, as he sees himself, to be depressed and find no comfort in trees and flowers and sunsets. He recalls his depression vividly and, like Capote, makes much of what many might think something less. But his many dead ride with him and, as with alcoholism, you can't know his clinical depression unless you've been there. No words match the blackness. It's not just a lot of simpering literary description Proust whips up.

The passage from Proust, aside from its contents and Proust's pleasure in writing it at the end of his huge novel, has a rich artistic purpose. The train journey leading up to this scene relaxes the reader, lays him out flat with Marcel's clinical ramblings. These are the calm before the "turn," the coming of knowledge, the pivotal scene of a big party at the Guermantes mansion in which all of Marcel's society is seen in old age and moral disrepair. Talking about his gloom and lack of literary talent, his stupor, the crazed, drained flatness of his soul, allows him in the passage above to rise to great heights of vivid spiritual contrast, more so than if—packed with well-being and great energy—he'd left the sanitorium and bounced up onto the train. To be sure, he enters the mansion having been struck by a bolt and dazed with release from his depression. He joins the party inspired and we receive his inspiration's fruits, not the sights and thoughts of mere energized well-being. He is above feeling good. He's inspired. Genius is flowing.

Think of it, you slip on a stone, catch yourself, and a two-year depression lifts. *I am stupendous.* What release!

One of Proust's masters is Madame de Sévigné, a brilliant letter writer in seventeenth-century France, whose eye for the social life and customs of her day and for the court of Louis XIV he treasured greatly. Her fourteen volumes of letters run even longer than his masterwork. Many of her letters were to her spoiled daughter, who shared very little of herself with her mother. What Proust loved in her, however, was less her sharp eye than the wholeheartedness and spirited personality behind her letters, as well as her skill at seeing both sides of a question. On her forty-sixth birthday she wrote to her daughter with her eyes "streaming, no matter how hard I try to hold back the tears." Her tears are for not having seen her newly married daughter for a whole year, a passion much like Proust's for his mother when he said: "One loves only what one cannot wholly possess." Proust's monstrous Baron de Charlus quotes Madame de Sévigné to Marcel, Proust's hero: "The important thing in life is not what one loves but that one loves."

Her daughter answers her coolly. Languishing, Madame de Sévigné answers her:

You ask me, my dear child, whether I still love life so well. I admit that it holds some searing sorrows. But I am even more dismayed at the thought of death. It seems to me so horrible that death is our only release from the ills of the world that if I could turn time backward, I would ask for nothing better: I find myself in an untenable position, set upon a course which distresses me: I was launched upon this life, though not of my own volition. I must leave this life, and that thought shatters me. And how will I leave it? By what door? When will it be? In what manner? Will I suffer a thousand and one agonies which will bring me to my death in desperation? Will I suffer a stroke of apoplexy? Will I die in an accident? How will I appear in the sight of God? Will it be fear and extremity which will turn me back to Him? Will I feel no other emotion but fear? What can I hope for? Am I worthy of Paradise? Is Hell my just desert? What an alternative! What a perplexity! . . . [H]ad I been consulted, I would have chosen to die in the arms of my nurse. That would have spared me much anguish and ensured me a sure passage to Heaven. But let us talk of other things. . . .

—*Madame de Sévigné: A Life and Letters* (1983),
Frances Mossiker

Great writers love to try their skill at describing death, much as actors measure their greatness with death scenes. Knowing that a character must die (Brünnhilde in flames, Violetta's last cough!) is always a weight on your heart, not just a favorable time to show off. Think how well Robert Stone shows us that frozen girl in the beer cooler. Superb skill! Stone's deepest feeling, however, lies in the priest's reeling back "in spiritual shock." You and I feel little more than abstract pity for that girl's dead eye. Death has to be charged with passion for us, with Stone's passion, by letting us experience it through the rum-drinking priest. As in movies, it's the reaction shot that dramatizes the writer's feelings, not the dying body. Tolstoy's *The Death of Ivan Ilych* stays with the body—but who feels anything for Ivan? Not I.

My feelings about Madame de Sévigné's letter fight each other as I imagine the reaction shot in her daughter. The mother wants her daughter to think wisely about death: I'm impressed by the finely cut phrases, but dismayed by what they say. Maybe in French her fourth sentence makes more sense— or Frances Mossiker has slipped in her Englishing of it. Madame de Sévigné says it's unfair ("horrible") that death is our only release from searing sorrows and the world's ills, and then: "if I could turn time backward, I would ask for nothing better." She wants *more* sorrow and ills? To me it seems that she's been seduced by her rhythms and that we're looking at a first draft that says less than is felt, and even falls into false self-questionings. Ah! you loved that letter—you hate me for saying these things! Go right ahead. I too write lame first drafts all the time, why shouldn't she? Hell, you should see the utterly clear-minded Tolstoy's first drafts—fantastic messes! When I typed up this letter, I was in Madame de Sévigné's spell throughout and even found life in what otherwise I'd skim as banalities, words and questions that really are dead on the page. Frankly, typing her letter is a deeper experience than merely reading it and drifting with her not uncommon feelings. Death is so phantomish to her that she avoids its most common qualities and impresses on her daughter her fears—fears based on a Catholic upbringing. I'm a non-Catholic who was raised in the Catholic church and few things strike me more leadenly than a received belief in heaven and hell and God's judgment after we die. If we're not in heaven and hell right now and being judged in the middle of our actions when we can do something about them, forget it. I'll take death, having given my all to life. But that's just me, I dig Whitman more than Jesus. This made clear, you will understand my delight when Madame de Sévigné finds herself in "an untenable position" and asks "Will it be fear and extremity which will turn me back to Him?" And I cry, Go with it, endure the fear and extremities and see where they take you—don't cave in, Madame S.! But she's soon digging back under the Rock. "Am I worthy of Paradise? Is Hell my just desert? What an alternative! What a perplexity!" Perplexity about what? Once again, her rhythms mislead her; she's just out to impress her daughter with underlinings of the thought. It's nothing we can understand, so we should just accept what we're taught. A lot of false piety.

Madame de Sévigné fears disturbing her flow as she writes; if the flow is right, the sense is assured. But this just ain't so. There are very few first drafts that don't bloom more strongly by having words replanted and whole sentences yanked out root and hairs. We fear that that dropped word or lost sentence will turn a sentence or paragraph lumpen. First thoughts, first thoughts are so fresh! Lively! Spontaneous! And mushy. They can be even fresher, more vivid, more springy if we rake out the rubbish. But Madame de Sévigné has a veiled purpose behind her tears over being parted from her daughter and her death fears: the moral education of her daughter. And while she may wave toward searing sorrows, the horrible, and her passing estrangement from Him, I think she offers her daughter a weaker, not a stronger, spiritual strength when she allows her fears to lead her to the idea that death right after birth would be her greatest happiness and ensure her "a sure passage to Heaven." This really is witless and no help at all for her daughter. If smothering babies made God happy, we wouldn't be here, would we?— nor would her daughter. What's right about her inane remark is that her fatalism leads toward a spiritual rebirth beyond dogma. If she goes with it, works her way through her fatalism instead of going back to sleep in the arms of a body of received religious ideas, she might have a breakthrough won through personal testing that would give new spiritual intensity both to her and her Church. The psalm says, I have walked through the valley of the shadow of death and I will fear no evil. Fatalism grants power to evil and is nothing to teach your daughter. Not inspiring at all.

Charlotte Mew, a spinster British poet (1869–1928) who swallowed no humbug, once said, upon seeing a dead rat:

> *I remember one evening of a long past Spring*
> *Turning in at a gate, getting out of a cart, and finding a*
> *   large dead rat in the mud of the drive.*
> *I remember thinking: alive or dead, a rat was a god-*
> *   forsaken thing,*
> *But at least, in May, that even a rat should be alive.*

> —"The Trees Are Down,"
> *Collected Poems of Charlotte Mew* (1953)

Mew is a great death (or life) poet whose flat statements move me far more than Madame de Sévigné's. Does Mew believe in an afterlife? I doubt it. The bulk of her poetry, poem after graveyard poem, shows her bitter about God. In "Madeleine in Church" she tells us "And He has never shared with me my haunted house . . . with its ghosts that have not any eyes for tears . . ." In fact, Miss Mew, a Christian with a leaning toward Catholicism who never converted, ended her life by swallowing a bottle of disinfectant. She never married because she feared passing on the taint of madness in her family—a younger brother and sister died in asylums. She tells us also in "Madeleine in Church":

> *I do not envy Him His victories,*
> *His arms are full of broken things.*

She told one friend that she sensed a "God of final peace at the heart of things." I love her. And her poetry. Such fearlessness at speaking her piece! I seldom dare speak that frankly in this book—or elsewhere. Mew had no faith in Man, only in trusted friends. But she was a gay, loud little thing, despite the blackness of her poems and the twisted broken threads of her smile behind them. Many disliked her. Today she's never anthologized, almost forgotten. A shadow in a lost apartment, she wavers before her gas-burner, her long lines breaking rules and drifting outward like the dawn. Death by being ignored can't subdue her breath. Why, if I lay my mind to hers, her gray lips will quiver and redden, and that old, odd smile of hers show death is a fraud. Her writing wakes the dead.

Hello, Charlotte! Tea? Time to wake up.

Ah, you've put on the pot? She smiles. Why have you been away so long?

Don't be a big scold, I haven't been anywhere. I just went out for some milk. And to look for a copy of your *Collected Poems* you might sign for me.

Oh, I'm in print again?

There you go, pulling at the traces. No, you're not in print. You're in my blood, that's what you are. So just put that in your bonnet and keep quiet about getting reprinted. I've been talking to myself all night about your long line and you've been quiet. What have you got to say for yourself?

I can't break out of my dreams.

Well, have a nip of this. It's raspberry flavored. Now, you can't fool me. You weren't asleep. You were just pretending— and you pretend pitifully. Someday I'm going to get very mad at you and beat the drum for your revival. Then you'll see how much peace you have.

Please, don't. I'm very comfortable just where I am.

In shadows, darling?

In shadow.

Well, I don't want those poems in shadow forever. I want the world interested in my girlfriend. I want her gay and loud, not a lost shadow.

No. Please don't bring me back to life. I can't stand that anymore.

Is that why you drank the disinfectant? Couldn't take the gaff? Sorry to disappoint you, Charlotte, but I'm your after-life—or part of it.

I thought I'd be at peace.

You're at peace, but I'm very much alive and have a totally different view of you than you do. What's more, we've been invited out. To dinner.

We have!

I have someone who wants to meet her big rival. So put on a fresh dickey and let's go.

Stop clowning around. How could I be anyone's rival?

My pet, you tell me things I've always wanted to know, and you tell me them better than anybody else. She wants to learn your little tricks. So drink up.

I wish I could get buried!

My, my! Now isn't that sad? But being buried isn't something you can hurry into, Charlotte. You've got to work up to it gradually. So let's be off.

Talk like that goes on all the time around my house. Dead people forever walk in on me. And living writers too, I'm not always among the dead. Not yet, anyway.

Mew's long line, of course, comes from Whitman, whose death elegies are many and glorious. I restrain myself and quote a short one, about a dead whore he's seen in the Philadelphia morgue, the city dead-house. Watch how the real action, despite the intensifying detail, takes place in the reaction shot in Whitman himself:

By the city dead-house by the gate,
As idly sauntering wending my way from the clangor,
I curious pause, for lo, an outcast form, a poor dead
      prostitute brought,
Her corpse they deposit unclaim'd, it lies on the damp
      brick pavement,
The divine woman, her body, I see the body, I look on it
      alone,
That house once full of passion and beauty, all else I
      notice not,
Nor stillness so cold, nor running water from faucet, nor
      odors morbific impress me,
But the house alone—that wondrous house—that deli-
      cate fair house—that ruin!
That immortal house more than all the rows of dwellings
      ever built!
Or white-domed capitol with majestic figure surmounted,
      or all the old high-spired cathedrals,
That little house alone more than all—poor, desperate
      house!
Fair, fearful wreck—tenement of a soul—itself a soul,
Unclaim'd, avoided house—take one breath from my
      tremulous lips,
Take one tear dropt aside as I go for thought of you,

Dead house of love—house of madness and sin, crumbled,
   crush'd,
 House of life, erewhile talking and laughing—but ah,
   poor house, dead even then,
 Months, years, an echoing, garnish'd house—but dead,
   dead, dead.

—"The City Dead-House" (1867–1881),
Leaves of Grass, Walt Whitman

 He wavers toward sentimentality but recovers with great power. We also question the line of inversions: "Nor stillness so cold, nor running water from faucet, nor odors morbific . . ." but Whitman doesn't question the line, which seems pitched too high for its matter as if ennobling the dead whore with a mock Miltonic voice. But much redeems the line, especially Whitman's following "Nor stillness so cold" with the hauntingly shallow and echoing "nor running water from faucet," a sound we hear but which cannot break her stillness. And he wants "odors morbific," the stinks of death wafting from morbific, not the flatness of "morbid odors." The line anchors the scene in sound and smell, the corpse on that hard, red "damp brick pavement," before Whitman holds up his grand, deeply felt likenings of her to houses and the majestic white-domed capitol with figure surmounted. He finds greater majesty in her ruin. We never get a description of her or suggestion of her background. All turns on the word "dead" which, counting the intriguing title, tolls eight times. This woman is as dead as Charlotte Mew's rat. Every dead body is dead in its own way and this one's not just dead, it's in ruins. And has been for years.

How does Whitman get this effect? First he disarms us, shows himself sauntering by the city gate, away from the clangor, idle, then suddenly curious about an outcast form. And here begins his unrivaled descriptive flow: outcast, poor dead prostitute, unclaim'd, divine (this shocks us), once full of passion and beauty, stillness, stinking with odors morbific, wondrous, delicate, fair, ruin, immortal, little, alone, poor, desperate, fair, fearful wreck, unclaim'd (twice!), avoided, dead, house of madness and sin, crumbled, crush'd, house of life, talking, laughing, poor, dead, echoing, garnish'd, dead, dead, dead. No doubt Whitman's notebook has a long list of feeling-words to choose from for this poem (he did that), but his deepest genius flows from his most feelingful word for this whore, "dead," and he drives it in like tent stakes around her, keeping the poem emotionally tense despite its big lines. Lines that grip and tear the sheets off your bed. What's all this that you own?

Part of the poem's success is its surprise, the way his tears and tremulous lips and other false releases suggest feeling without driving it home. (That tear is "dropt aside as I go"—perhaps wiped off with a finger—it's dropped on the corpse as he gives her his psychic kiss.) He withholds the real release for the end, not wanting you to beat him to it too early. You admire his strong likenesses of her to rows of dwelling houses and the domed capitol, the high-spired cathedrals, the little house, the fair, fearful wreck—the "house" he mentions thirteen times with never a forced repeat. But what at last wins us is the triple "dead, dead, dead," which seems to carry us beyond poetry. Just as King Lear's howl over Cordelia bespeaks his shock,

No, no, no life!
Why should a dog, a horse, a rat, have life,

And thou no breath at all? Thou'lt come no more,
Never, never, never, never, never!

and fills us with pity for his horror and loss—a beloved daughter sucked away into absolute nothingness—so Whitman drums his "dead, dead, dead" with equal force but does not arrive at horror. Like the dead whore, Cordelia dies offstage, but it makes no difference. Death itself is unfelt. Only Whitman and Lear feel. They get the reaction shot. In *Hamlet* Ophelia dies offstage; Gertrude's soliloquy "There is a willow grows aslant the brook" tries to sway us but fails, being too sweet and out of tone with suicide, *especially* after Hamlet's suicide aria "To be or not to be." Only the anger of Ophelia's brother Laertes as he attacks Hamlet by her grave gives any bite to Ophelia's death—though the sight of her singing beautiful, sex-riddled lyrics while mad hangs in the air.

There's much more to be said about Whitman's whore. He calls her divine, wondrous, delicate fair, a house of love, a house of life, and he opens our eyes to the immense loss in those dead limbs, then turns against our expectations and tells us she's been dead for months, years, and was only an echoing, garishly dressed house when she died. We would call that great poetic ingenuity on his part, but that in poem after poem he works against our expectations and shocks us with feelings much greater than we thought likely from any of his subjects. If you have *Leaves of Grass,* read "This Compost," about a pile of cowshit, and see what he does with something that unpromising. He makes that manure pile biblical. No, he makes it himself, Whitman the pile of manure, the compost heap. He hasn't said he's one with the grass for nothing. He is Walt, whose pages are grass. He is the earth itself, a great globe of manure worked over and over with sour dead, hot and ripe with diseased corpses rotting within him, Whitman is all mites and foul meat, and yet he is the bean bursting noiselessly through the mold in the garden, the delicate spear of the onion piercing upward, yes, he is beans and onions:

> *Now I am terrified at the Earth, it is that calm and*
> *   patient,*
> *It grows such sweet things out of such corruptions,*
> *It turns harmless and stainless on its axis, with such*
> *   endless successions of diseas'd corpses,*
> *It distills such exquisite winds out of such infused fetor,*
> *It renews with such unwitting looks its prodigal, annual,*
> *   sumptuous crops,*
> *It gives such divine materials to men, and accepts such*
> *   leavings from them at last.*

> —"This Compost" (1856–1881), *Leaves of Grass,* Walt Whitman

Fearless Walt is all his characters, even cowshit.

Tennessee Williams loves to stop a scene in midflight and give a character (himself, of course) an aria, and some of these are more moving than the play they're in. In the aria below, Val, a wandering guitarist sometimes known as Snakeskin because of his jacket, tries to woo Lady out of the darkness of her marriage to the ruler of the underworld, Jabe. The play *Orpheus Descending* was filmed as *The Fugitive Kind,* with Marlon Brando and Anna Magnani as Val and Lady. Brando gives his aria a reading of passionate understatement that lets the words bloom:

> VAL: You know they's a kind of bird that don't have legs so it can't light on nothing but has to stay all its life on its wings in the sky? That's true. I seen one once, it had died and fallen to earth and it was light-blue colored and its body was tiny as your little finger, that's the truth, it had a body as tiny as your little finger and so light on the palm of your hand it didn't weigh more than a feather, but its wings spread out this wide but they was transparent, the color of the sky and you could see through them. That's what they call protection coloring. Camouflage, they call it. You can't tell those birds from the sky and that's why the hawks don't catch them, don't see them up there in the high blue sky near the sun! . . . They fly so high in gray weather the God-dam hawks would get dizzy. But those little birds, they don't have no legs at all and they live their whole lives on the wing, and they sleep on the wind, that's how they sleep at night, they just spread their wings and go to sleep on the wind like other birds fold their wings and go to sleep on a tree. They sleep on the wind and never light on this earth but one time when they die! . . . So'd I like to be one of those birds; they's lots of people would like to be one of those birds and never be—corrupted!

> —*Orpheus Descending* (1955), Tennessee Williams

When Williams first wrote this play in 1940, as *Battle of Angels,* myth gripped his imagination, especially the story of Orpheus (or Hermes or Mercury) going into the underworld to rescue Persephone, who had been kidnapped by and married to Pluto, ruler of darkness. With Persephone's return, spring would bloom on earth. The play closed in Boston. In revising it later as *Orpheus Descending,* he saw that in the first version he'd not written a speech whose beauty made Val ring true as Orpheus. That big lack inspires this aria.

Does it work? On the page it shines—in the theater, and particularly in the film, it sings. Poems in plays and movies always hearten an audience, even lesser poems than this one. They often add a distinguished moment to otherwise foot-slogging works. When in doubt, sing. As in opera, song makes everything larger than life, dramatizes feelings that can't be shown realistically. Williams, by the way, cribs his bird from Whitman's masterful "To the Man-of-War-Bird," a poem about a real seabird that is ever in flight and sleeps on the wind.

Val and Lady envy the bird, although this bird is Val's own valiant heart and its wings are song. We are all of our characters! The dead whore in "The City Dead-House" is Whitman himself, which is perhaps why he leaves her featureless, or cannot bear looking at her face. Val longs to rise above his futureless career as a solo blues player at New Orleans parties and have his spirit become not a blues but an inspired bird whose whole life is spent in the sky. Up from death, beyond the blues.

But I'm just riffing. Don't take all this with a stone face and just nod your head. I talk to myself but don't sit around cutting up books for inspiration. You don't need a book to get writing. You need a wind within. And, hard times help. Funny how we all write best with our backs to the wall. "Agonies are one of my changes of garments," Whitman says. It's amazing what inspired him. Read his "Prayer of Columbus" if you want to know how he wrote about his stroke and paralysis. Disablement squeezed the living daylight into his line. Val, too, the wandering bluesman, fights paralysis with song.

Edith Wharton fought social paralysis with prose. She started writing out of boredom with her high-society friends, who were hidebound, blank-eyed cows. Timid, private spirits, without even the energy for business. Moneyed Philistines, suspicious of the arts. But she painted them richly. Critic Edmund Wilson calls her "the poet of interior decoration," which is unfair. But see for yourself as she describes operagoers at Lower Manhattan's Academy of Music in the early 1870s. She starts with the singers in *Faust,* as M. Capoul (Faust) tries to woo shy, virginal Madame Nilsson (Marguerite) into a bedroom. In a box, Newland Archer glances at nearby May Welland, his bride-to-be, and tells himself that virginal May is as sexually witless as Marguerite and has no idea what Faust is after in the bedroom:

And he contemplated her absorbed young face with a thrill of possessorship in which pride in his own masculine initiation was mingled with a tender reverence for her abysmal purity. . . . He did not in the least wish the future Mrs. Newland Archer to be a simpleton. He meant her (thanks to his enlightening companionship) to develop a social tact and readiness of wit enabling her to hold her own with the most popular married women of the "younger set," in which it was the recognised custom to attract masculine homage while playfully discouraging it. . . .

How this miracle of fire and ice was to be created, and to sustain itself in a harsh world, he had never taken the time to think out; but he was content to hold his view without analysing it, since he knew it was that of all the carefully brushed, white-waistcoated, buttonhole-flowered gentlemen who succeeded each other in the club box, exchanged friendly greeting with him, and turned their opera glasses critically on the circle of ladies who were the product of the system.

Wharton now shows us Lawrence Lefferts, the foremost authority on "form" in New York:

One had only to look at him, from the slant of his bald forehead and the curve of his beautiful fair moustache to the long patent-leather feet at the other end of his lean and elegant person, to feel that the knowledge of "form" must be congenital in anyone who knew how to wear such good clothes so carelessly and carry such height with so much lounging grace. . . . And on the question of pumps versus patent-leather "oxfords" his authority had never been disputed.

—*The Age of Innocence* (1920), Edith Wharton

When I was ten my mother and I moved from Erie and went to live with a man of great social standing in nearby Jamestown. At last a house of our own. One winter afternoon, home alone, I went down to look over our cellar's wines and whiskeys, our coal pile, our huge furnace with its great glowing bed that put a spell on me. Then Mother came home from the Town Club to make supper. "Oh my God, what is that stink!" She sniffed about the kitchen and the hot-air heater near the living room. "March in here! My son, did you do you-know-what in the furnace?"

Questions like that never sneak up on us in a Wharton novel. Social poise is all. At the opera Newland Archer and his friend Mr. Sillerton Jackson soon find themselves stunned by the return to society of Countess Ellen Olenska, who wears a diamond Josephine headdress and a rather theatrical and bosomy dark blue velvet gown. Ellen is rumored to have bolted from her brutal husband, Count Olenska, with his male secretary, from whom she later parted and then lived alone in Venice. We first see her as a worldly-wise Garboesque, perhaps fallen, woman. Although Newland Archer has that very afternoon become engaged to the innocent May Welland, whose blush rises up her bosom and cheeks, he soon falls in love with Countess Olenska and her direct ironies, and enters a strange unreality pursuing her as his mistress. A lusty plot? Well, their rare meetings reach only the first kiss before moral ties split them. They do share a private room at an inn outside Boston but this is not Wharton's sly way of saying they went to bed together. This is not the ecstatic reunion in *Anna Karenina* with Anna pressing Vronsky's hands to her breasts, saying, "Yes, you have taken possession of me, and I am yours." Not that scene.

Wharton's voice changes throughout the novel, is ploddingly ironic in the passages above, later quite trim in scenes of greater intensity. At the opera, she fills a wide canvas with portraiture and dense social detail: Newland Archer is smug and lofty, and plans to educate May about seduction by reading *Faust* to her on the Italian lakes. Simpleton no more, she must be "worldly-wise" and as eager to please as Countess Olenska— a thought Wharton smiles at, calling the remodeled May-to-be a "miracle of fire and ice." Newland Archer (always the full name) doesn't worry about how this wondrous upgrading of May's wit will take place: every carefully brushed gentleman can train a mare to jump. For that matter, he's the most worldly of all his club's specimens of gentility. Can passion save this suave dolt?

Lawrence Lefferts is New York's foremost authority on "form," she tells us, then adds wicked words about Lefferts's physical form, with his slant bald forehead and curved fair moustache matched by patent-leather shoes "at the other end of his lean and elegant person." Other end, hmm. The absolute authority on patent-leather oxfords is an ass?

With the entrance of Countess Olenska, who has just come from her sexual education in Europe, an erotic note heats the page. Wharton implies, This is a stultifying society we're in but I know about hot hands and secret lusts. As we find out, she knows also about the bear-trap grip of that society, the bull's horns that love can toss you about on, the pitfalls of logic in marriage when good sense fades before feeling (or lack of feeling), the psychic darkness gnawing with a shrew's teeth at our faith in love's empowerment of life, and how society fears that adultery and divorce can fatally infect its lifeblood. But I drift into litcrit.

Could Wharton's descriptions be better written? I think so. But she attacks her subjects from a height that strengthens her irony. There's no waffling about or softening of what she sees. Her hero is a prig among prigs (or prick among pricks, as women might write today). He will grow and at least try hopelessly to yank himself out of the social concrete fast-holding him to marriage with a weak-minded society dame. I quail only at a handful of worn-out phrases, and words that could be En-glished for greater intensity. Sharper words could give a blood-ier cut: "And he contemplated her absorbed young face with a thrill of possessorship in which pride in his own masculine initiation was mingled with tender reverence for her abysmal purity"—I'd improve that as: "And he dwelled on her sucking young eyes with a thrill of ownership in which his readiness to deflower mingled with a tender reverence for her abysmal pu-rity." If you don't like "sucking," try "rapt young eyes": either beats "absorbed young face." And so on. You may not agree but I think she needs prodding out of a slog of quilled-pen journal-ese. Wharton enjoys to the hilt her recovery of operagoing in her youth. But she'd have more fun if she'd pick up her pace, let her words trot and speak to the point. Screw fine prose—it dies!

Let's read some writing that does move. In *Young Men and Fire,* Norman Maclean in very old age tells us about a forest fire from his Montana youth. Maclean had been a Smokejumper who parachuted onto the edges of fires and helped dig trenches that stopped a fire's advance. He did not help in this particular fire he tells about, but he recalls it as a great tragedy in which only three of fifteen Smokejumpers came out alive. Thirteen died almost within seconds of each other. The writing may seem "mere journalism," but it's not. Maclean brings great force to this tragedy, especially in his later thoughts about the depths of pride and compassion in the dead Smokejumpers.

First he tells us about two kinds of fire so we'll be able to follow this fire in its deviltry. The worst danger in a ground fire is that it become a "crown fire"—a fire that explodes among interlacing branches of trees close together. A crown fire can become so intense that it ignites distant trees beyond a clearing without first burning a path to them. Far trees just explode. "Fire whirls" are when flames whirl and roar in unstable air and little "dust devils" unite into a tornado that breaks the sound barrier and causes new fires. Fire whirls have a downdraft down the center, a vortex caused by lack of oxygen, whose outer ring is an updraft that can reach the edge of the atmosphere. Some giant fire whirls pick up burning logs and, throwing them, start spot fires far ahead of the fire's path. In the incident Maclean tells about, some firefighters find themselves trapped between two fires. They are ringed by fire. They hope that they can climb to the top ridge of a gulch and get past the fire. But they are in a death trap, shut out from all the world but the ridge above them.

> [T]hey could see what it is really not possible to see: the center of a blowup. It is really not possible to see the center of a blowup because the smoke only occasionally lifts, and when it does all that can be seen are pieces, pieces of death flying around looking for you—burning cones, branches circling on wings, a log in flight without a propeller. Below in the bottom of the gulch was a great roar without visible flames but blown with winds on fire. Now, for the first time, they could have seen to the head of the gulch if they had been looking that way. And now, for the first time, to their left the top of the ridge was visible, looking when the smoke parted to be not more than two hundred yards away.
>
>   . . . Sallee said, "I saw him [Dodge] bend over and light a fire with a match. I thought, With the fire almost on our back, what the hell is the boss doing lighting another fire in front of us?"

It shouldn't be hard to imagine just what most of the crew must have thought when they first looked across the open hillside and saw their boss seemingly playing with a matchbook in dry grass. . . . Sallee repeated, "We thought he must have gone nuts." A few minutes later his fire became more spectacular still, when Sallee, having reached the top of the ridge, looked back and saw the foreman enter his own fire and lie down in its hot ashes to let the main fire pass over him.

— *Young Men and Fire* (1992), Norman Maclean

This amazing event, the foreman starting a fire in the path of a blowup, and then lying down in its embers, becomes one of the great questions Maclean tries to answer. Some fifteen minutes later, Dodge, the foreman, rises alive from the embers, the main fire having passed him by because he'd burned all the fuel it might have used, bringing its explosive temperatures with it. Those temperatures never reached Dodge because of his wiliness. The question is, Did his fire rush upslope and kill the climbers above and at the same time cut off climbers racing upward from below? No hard answer is possible but Maclean makes an educated guess in favor of Dodge.

Aside from mounting excitement, what grips us about these passages is Maclean's clear eye and flow of clear words. When you think of the boiling masses he's shaping for us to sense in outline, you see the hard task he sets himself. Twelve of the men climbing the last two hundred yards suffocate, fall, try to rise and later are found burned and stretching toward the top of the ridge. Maclean studies every yard of their tragedy.

Is this writing faultless? I think it is. Its refusal to sentimentalize or overdraw the men's deaths lets us experience the dying men's last thoughts very much as they must have been. Maclean's extrafine remaking of the events leads to some mystical notes: "As you fail, you sink back in the region of strange gases and red and blue darts where there is no oxygen and here you die in your lungs; then you sink in prayer into the main fire that consumes. . . ."

Hard to beat that.

Anaïs Nin wrote the first paragraph below in her very first diary, in 1914, when she was eleven. When she reclaimed this entry in 1948 for her story "Winter of Artifice, Part 1: Djuna" in *Under a Glass Bell,* she was forty-five:

August 12. Yesterday we reached New York . . . New York is big, with buildings of 20, 19 or 17 stories on each side of the street. . . . [W]e took the train to Kew. It is beautiful! In the country, pretty houses with little gardens, flowers, small neat white streets. Among the houses was my aunt's house. My little cousin Nuna was at the door and in a few minutes we were friends. I made a little garden, I played, I swung in a swing and tried to ride a bicycle. I rediscovered my little house in Cuba, my dream, a villa surrounded by fields, flowers, a little garden, all white furniture, order, and something in all this that one cannot explain . . . Maman sings, I admire everything, I think to myself that I am in a foreign land, I watch my cousins and brothers playing, and finally I think I will leave my diary to go and play too.

August 13. Description of heaven on earth. Green lawns strewn with flowers, tiny houses, little white roads neatly designed, a few trees, bright sunshine, small gardens full of flowers. My Aunt Edelmira's house is arranged in exquisite taste, white furniture, everything is small, nice, very clean and orderly. A swing, bicycles, a nice little girl cousin, a friendly boy cousin, a good kind aunt whom no one could help loving. I have to say hurrah for Kew Gardens, hurrah for the house, hurrah for my aunt, hurrah for the flowers and the fields, hurrah for God who has sent us to this earthly Paradise.

—*Linotte: The Early Diary of Anaïs Nin 1914–1920*,
translated from the French by Jean L. Sherman

Please remember all those hurrahs as we read the rewrite:

They entered New York harbor, her mother, her two brothers and she, in the midst of a violent thunderstorm. The Spaniards aboard the ship were terrified; some of them were kneeling in prayer. They had reason to be terrified,—the bow of the ship had been struck by lightning. . . .

She was eleven years old. Her mother was absent most of the day searching for work. There were socks to darn and dishes to wash. She had to bathe and dress her brothers. She had to amuse them, aid them with their lessons. The days were full of bleak effort in which great sacrifices were demanded of all of them . . . the color and the fragrance had gone out of their life. When she heard music, laughter and talk in the room where her mother gave singing lessons, she was saddened by the feeling of something lost.

And so, little by little, she shut herself up within the walls of her diary. . . .

The yearning for her father became a long, continuous plaint. Every page contained long pleas to him, invocations to God to reunite them. Hours and hours of suffocating moods, of dreams and reveries, of feverish restlessness, of morbid, somber memories and longings. She could not bear to listen to music, especially the arias her mother sang: "Ever since the day," "Some day he'll come," etc. Her mother seemed to choose only the songs which reminded her of him.

She felt crippled, lost, transplanted, rebellious. . . . New York was hostile, cold, indifferent. They were immigrants, and they were made to feel it. Even on Christmas Eve her mother had to sing at the church in order to earn a few pennies.

—"Winter of Artifice—Djuna," *Under a Glass Bell* (1948), Anaïs Nin

Nin's long-faced rewrite brings a large loss to the diary's gaga charm. Every childish sight rings with feeling while each middle-aged sentence clamps down on feeling, replacing her child's sense of a radiant new world with one of darkness and loss. Why? Two reasons: Her story "Winter of Artifice" has an artistic aim Nin knows the diary doesn't add to: to show how her stony, self-centered father's cold critical eye sapped her childhood and left her pale and sickly. And Nin has since then lived through World War I, tried to relieve her fear and hatred of sex when married by having herself surgically deflowered, mixed with artists in Paris, read widely among the surrealists and been touched by her lover Henry Miller's black surrealism, been given to fits of hysteria—and a lot more, including having split off mentally into a stony, self-centered, cold, critical Voice that relentlessly demands It reign in any striving for joy. The storm and storm and stress roll on and all turns fey and gloomy as she strangles her own childhood. "I have to say hurrah for Kew Gardens, hurrah for the house, hurrah for my aunt, hurrah for the flowers and the fields, hurrah for God who has sent us to this earthly Paradise." Stabbed through the chest.

And all for art!*

Now let's compare two more texts. One sultry summer day in London, Wild Bill Shakespeare, now forty-two and thickening, in moist clothes that smell of armpits and his privates, sits in some small back room or stuffy attic with little leaded windows and thick panes, and with a sharpened goose quill scratches out *Tony and Cleo,* a play about Italian shipping magnate Tony Verdi and his affair with Cleo Callas, the great star of Grauman's Egyptian Pictures, and as the afternoon fades, his ear still feeding streettalk into the shoptalk of his tragic giants, he wonders whether he should send to the confectioner's for some sweetmeats to clear his mind when suddenly arise before

---

*"No!" My in-house fan and critic, who knew Nin and edited a magazine piece of hers, defends the "Winter of Artifice" rewrite of *Linotte* on many grounds: young Anaïs, or Linotte, wrote her diary as a literary work for her absent father to read and in the beginning gives a sprightly life to her words; later, as the family falls into poverty, her writing turns more painful and Cinderella-like. Also, my diary quote covers her arrival, while "Winter of Artifice" compresses feelings from a larger period. In recollection, as Nin looked back on her youth, life was tough. In his preface to *Linotte,* Joaquin Nin-Culmell, Nin's brother, says: "Later she reinterpreted many events, many situations, many impressions. *Linotte* may seem to contradict these later interpretations, but I do not feel that this is so. After all, reality is many layered." My critic thinks I'm unfair, uncompassionate, and savage to a woman who broke free from her Latin background with its oppression of women and was a great pioneer of women's rights and admirable artist.

I think the diarist is honest, and the novelist bent on art.

him two eyes, alert and clever as blue-green scarabs but with two thousand years of royal Egyptian lineage alive in their date-colored depths—all Egypt moves in her glance, sways under lids of turquoise, in kohl-blackened lashes and whites of bright ivory—and he cries aloud, "I need a big aria about Cleo! Something *GORGEOUS*!" Spine shaking, he lights a candle stub and, turning to Plutarch's *Lives* open on a stool beside him, reads this:

Such being his temper, the last and crowning mischief that could befall him came in the love of Cleopatra. . . . He fell into the snare thus. When making preparation for the Parthian war, he sent to command her to make her personal appearance in Cilicia, to answer an accusation that she had given great assistance, in the late wars, to Cassius. Dellius, who was sent on this message, had no sooner seen her face, and remarked her adroitness and subtlety in speech, but he felt convinced that Antony would not so much as think of giving any molestation to a woman like this; on the contrary, she would be the first in favor with him. So he set himself at once to pay his court to the Egyptian, and gave her his advice, "to go . . . in her best attire," and bade her fear nothing from Antony, the gentlest and kindest of soldiers. She had some faith in the words of Dellius, but more in her own attractions; which, having formerly recommended her to Caesar and the young Caenus Pompey, she did not doubt might prove yet more successful with Antony. Their acquaintance was with her when a girl, young and ignorant of the world, but she was to meet Antony in the time of life when women's beauty is most splendid, and their intellects are in full maturity. She made great preparation for her journey, of money, gifts, and ornaments of value, such as so wealthy a kingdom might afford, but she brought with her her surest hopes in her own magic arts and charms.

She received several letters, both from Antony and from his friends, to summon her, but she took no account of these orders; and at last, as if in mockery of them, she came sailing up the river Cydnus, in a barge with gilded stern and out-spread sails of purple, while oars of silver beat time to the music of flutes and fifes and harps. She herself lay all along under a canopy of cloth of gold, dressed as Venus in a pic-ture, and beautiful young boys, like painted Cupids, stood on each side to fan her. Her maids were dressed like sea nymphs and graces, some steering at the rudder, some work-ing at the ropes. The perfumes diffused themselves from the vessel to the shore, which was covered with multitudes, part following the galley up the river on either bank, part run-ning out of the city to see her. The market-place was quite emptied, and Antony at last was left alone sitting upon the tribunal; while the word went through all the multitude, that Venus was come to feast with Bacchus, for the common good of Asia. On her arrival, Antony sent to invite her to supper. She thought it fitter he should come to her; so, will-ing to show his good-humor and courtesy, he complied, and went. He found the preparations to receive him magnificent beyond expression, but nothing so admirable as the great number of lights; for on a sudden there was let down alto-gether so great a number of branches with lights in them so ingeniously disposed, some in squares, and some in circles, that the whole thing was a spectacle that has seldom been equalled for beauty.

. . . She, perceiving that his raillery was broad and gross, and savored more of the soldier than the courtier, rejoined in the same taste, and fell into it at once, without any sort of reluctance or reserve. For her actual beauty, it is said, was not in itself so remarkable that none could be compared with her, or that no one could see her without being struck by it, but the contact of her presence, if you lived with her, was irresistible; the attraction of her person, joining with the charm of her conversation, and the character that attended all she said or did, was something bewitching. It was a pleasure merely to hear the sound of her voice, with which, like an instrument of many strings, she could pass from one language to another; so that there were few of the barbarian nations that she answered by an interpreter; to most of them she spoke herself, as to the Ethiopians, Troglodytes, Hebrews, Arabians, Syrians, Medes, Parthians, and many others, whose language she had learnt; which was all the more surprising because most of the kings, her forebears, scarcely gave themselves the trouble to acquire the Egyptian tongue, and several of them quite abandoned the Macedonian.

Antony was so captivated by her that [he suffered] himself to be carried away by her to Alexandria, there to keep holiday, like a boy, in play and diversion. . . . Philotas . . . used to tell my grandfather Lamprias that, having some acquaintance with one of the royal cooks, he was invited by him . . . to come and see the sumptuous preparations for supper. So he was taken into the kitchen, where he admired the prodigious variety of all things; but particularly, seeing eight wild boars roasting whole, says he, "Surely you have a great number of guests." The cook laughed at his simplicity, and told him there were not above twelve to sup, but that every dish was to be served up just roasted to a turn, and if anything was but one minute ill-timed, it was spoiled. "And," he said, "maybe Antony will sup just now, maybe not this hour, maybe he will call for wine, or begin to talk, and will put it off. So that," he continued, "it is not one, but many suppers must be had in readiness, as it is impossible to guess at his hour."

... To return to Cleopatra; Plato admits four sorts of flattery, but she had a thousand. Were Antony serious or disposed to mirth, she had at any moment new delight or charm to meet his wishes; at every turn she was upon him, and let him escape her neither by day nor by night. She played at dice with him, drank with him, hunted with him; and when he exercised in arms, she was there to see. At night she would go rambling with him to disturb and torment people at their doors and windows, dressed like a servant-woman, for Antony also went in servant's guise, and from these expeditions he often came home very scurvily answered, and sometimes even beaten severely, though most people guessed who it was. . . . It would be trifling without end to be particular in his follies. . . .

—"Antony," Plutarch's *Lives* (A.D. 105–115), Dryden translation, with Arthur Hugh Clough

Blots fly over the parchment as Wild Bill writes, his eyes gleaming at black words catching the candlelight before they dry:

MAECENUS: Welcome from Egypt, sir.
ENOBARBUS: Half the heart of Caesar, worthy Maecenus!
My honorable friend, Agrippa!
AGRIPPA: Good Enobarbus!
MAEC.: We have cause to be glad that matters are so well digested. You stayed well by't in Egypt.
ENO.: Ay, sir; we did sleep day out of countenance,
And made the night light with drinking.

MAEC.: Eight wild-boars roasted whole at a breakfast, and but twelve persons there; is this true?

ENO.: This was but as a fly by an eagle: we had much more monstrous matter of feast, which worthily deserved noting.

MAEC.: She's a most triumphant lady, if report be square with her.

ENO.: When she first met Mark Antony, she pursed up his heart, upon the river of Cydnus.

AGR.: There she appeared indeed, or my reporter devised well for her.

ENO.: I will tell you.

The barge she sat in, like a burnish'd* throne,
Burn'd on the water: the poop was beaten gold;
Purple the sails, and so perfumed that
The winds were love-sick with them; the oars were silver,
Which to the tune of flutes kept stroke and made
The water which they beat to follow faster,
As amorous of their strokes. For her own person,
It beggar'd all description: she did lie
In her pavilion, cloth-of-gold of tissue,
O'er-picturing that [painting of] Venus where we see
The fancy out-work nature: on each side her
Stood pretty dimpled boys, like smiling Cupids,
With divers-color'd fans, whose wind did seem
To glow the delicate cheeks which they did cool,
And what they undid did.

---

*These apostrophes make clear that the final -ed not be sounded, but the two-beat foot sometimes asks for the -ed to be sounded and at other times not. In "worthily deserved noting," I'd sound the -ed, and again in "pursed up his heart." In "there she appeared indeed" I wouldn't, but in "my reporter devised well" I would. Whitman too follows this rule; all those apostrophes of his are not classical decoration or weak-minded ennoblement of bad lines.

AGR.:   O, rare for Antony!

ENO.: Her gentlewomen, like the Nereides,
So many mermaids, tended her i' the eyes,
And made their bends adornings: at the helm
A seeming mermaid steers: The silken tackle
Swell with the touches of those flower-soft hands,
That yarely frame the office [nimbly keep the barge on
                              course]. From the barge
A strange invisible perfume hits the sense
Of the adjacent wharfs. The city cast
Her people out upon her; and Antony,
Enthroned i' the market-place, did sit alone,
Whistling to the air; which, but for vacancy,
Had gone to gaze on Cleopatra too,
And made a gap in nature.

AGR.:   Rare Egyptian!

ENO.: Upon her landing, Antony sent to her,
Invited her to supper: she replied,
It should be better he became her guest,
Which she entreated: our courteous Antony,
Whom ne'er the word of "No" woman heard speak,
Being barber'd ten times o'er, goes to the feast,
And, for his ordinary [meal], pays his heart
For what his eyes eat only.

AGR.:   Royal wench!

She made great Caesar lay his sword to bed:
He plough'd her, and she cropp'd.

ENO.:   I saw her once
Hop forty paces through the public street;
And having lost her breath, she spoke, and panted,
That she did make defect perfection,
And, breathless, power breathe forth.

MAEC.: Now Antony must leave her utterly.

ENO.: Never, he will not:
Age cannot wither her, nor custom stale
Her infinite variety: other women cloy
The appetites they feed, but she makes hungry
Where most she satisfies: for vilest things
Become themselves in her, that the holy priests
Bless her when she is riggish [angry].

—*Antony and Cleopatra* (Act II, Scene ii)
(1606), William Shakespeare

When she's poisonous and a complete bitch or worse, the priests bless Her Divine Vileness. Nice!

What do we hear in Wild Bill's rewriting of Plutarch? We're alerted quickly that this gossip of the gods worthily deserves reporting and "my reporter devised well for her." Maecenus and Agrippa are milking Enobarbus for hot tales from Alexandria, and Enobarbus gives them a golden shovelful. Shakespeare tells us from the top that this will be two-beat journalism and then sets to ripping off Plutarch so rapidly, he can barely slow down to make his lines scan. He may well have knocked off this scene in the time it took to pen the words, no rewriting—an hour's work. I remember when I first read this fifty years ago, I thought it engraved in gold, every syllable beaten finely in the goldshop in Shakespeare's brain. Who could envy genius that glowing? How could I know he was rewriting a news service item for the bulldog edition? Please don't think I question Wild Bill's gorgeous refinement of Plutarch as being less than genius. It's just that when the spirit is flowing, and Shakespeare finds his Plutarch white-hot and ready to pour, perhaps not even stopping to blot his blots, it's not quite the same as smelting down completely imaginary details from ore from your own mine. When you are up there in the heavens of invention, you don't overrefine, you turn out three or four canvases a day, like Picasso, or three or four scenes before dinner, like Wild Bill, fueled by enthusiasm, using your accidents, and relying on a kind of drunken rightness to each stroke. Of course, even when revising for the academy, as in his sonnets, he tries for a loose, easy line, nothing too worked over. This is not to say his mouth didn't fill with ecstatic saliva when he wrote

> The barge she sat in, like a burnish'd throne,
> Burn'd on the water: the poop was beaten gold;
> Purple the sails, and so perfumed that
> The winds were love-sick with them; the oars were silver,
> Which to the tune of flutes kept stroke and made
> The water which they beat to follow faster,
> As amorous of their strokes. . . .

His inventions on the lovesick winds and amorous water whorls lapping after the silver oars are his own spicings, some might say purple pen, not Plutarch's. But these ecstatic details are just the quality that first draws us to Shakespeare, as the gazelle-eyed virgin on the cigar box draws us to our first Havanas. *Ohhh,* smell that cedar! He sees the commonplace with enlarging simplicity. Perhaps we are first drawn to him when the blood is racing and we are young and green and sit back amazed at what he sees in a mouse, or death, or in memories, and plays on us with the rich cello strokes of his sonnets— "When to the sessions of sweet silent thought, I summon up remembrance of things past . . ."—and slowly we sink into the body of received ideas and scholarship about Shakespeare, who fades into SHAKESPEARE.

Since this is a book about inspiration, I'll tell you why I make jokes about Shakespeare. Tolstoy when writing about *King Lear* was so upset by meeting a reputation as big as his own that he used a voice of heavy nitpicking to rip into *Lear* as so much wastepaper. I face a playwright whose fame is so universal, who has been so studied and remade by each generation of readers, and whose glories feed from one play into another in our experience of the poet, that we can no longer hear his lines as he wrote them. I spoke of "Wild Bill" first of all because writing this book is fun but also to help slip affectionately behind his fame and show the simplicity, almost raggedness of his lines. So much of his greatest work is simply written! The legalese of "To be or not to be; that is the question"; the slow footsteps of "Tomorrow and tomorrow and tomorrow"; the speech of Lear over Cordelia: "Why should a dog, a horse, a rat, have life"; Othello's "Farewell the big wars"; Antony's "Friends, Romans, countrymen"; Prospero's "Our revels now are ended"—the first quality that should strike us about these famous passages is the use of simple words to carry large feelings. With plays, Shakespeare did not have time to overwrite. He didn't think of each work as a big literary artifice that called for the Atlas-like labors of Thomas Mann lifting up *The Magic Mountain*. He had five acts sketched out in his mind with a few key words, charged in, and within five minutes of writing the first scene surrendered to his unconscious to bring up what Plutarch or Holinshed couldn't supply him with. Only in *Antony and Cleopatra* does he let loose and strike out into the unknown with so many gorgeously surreal passages, such as Cleopatra's lament as Antony dies:

> O, see, my women,
> The crown o' the earth doth melt. My lord!
> O, withered is the garland of the war,
> The soldier's pole is fall'n: young boys and girls
> Are level now with men; the odds is gone,
> And there is nothing left remarkable
> Beneath the visiting moon. (Act IV, Scene iv)

Sometimes unfamiliar words or baffled editors wrongly weighing a comma or lines mangled in the First Folio make him hard to follow. But so what. Just remember that everything in the play, even the knotty parts, is Shakespeare and he has invited you into his mind to enjoy his creations: he is the barge, the silver oars, the pretty dimpled boys, the eight wild boars roasting, Antony sitting alone in the marketplace whistling to himself, and he is Cleopatra, whom age cannot wither, nor custom stale in his infinite variety. Also, the barge does double duty as characterization. Cleopatra is the barge, its purple sail and silken tackle that answers yarely to flower-soft fingers, and she is the strange invisible perfume spreading out to the wharfs. That's all her, and he knows it even if Plutarch doesn't, just as she is the wandering moon with nothing left remarkable beneath it. She is the whole universe of the poem and all the other characters, including Antony, are foils for a poet's eye gripped by her Egyptian sun and moon and kohl-blackened lashes under turquoise lids and date-colored eyes set in whites of ivory. That she will be played by a treble-voiced boy with two oranges in his star-blue Egyptian costume adds something we'll never know to Shakespeare's thoughts.

Antony and Cleopatra is all color and richness. But first of all he hears the silence of listeners into whom he pours his voices and for whom he measures his line and makes each voice clear. Does the voice or the line come first? I'd say the voice comes to be his main support, though like any writer he begins drugged by the music of verse and in his early plays writes many over-crowded lines seeking to sound the sublimity of English verse. But the need to speak directly to his audience at last wins out over the heaviness and excess of straining for the sublime line. Once conscious striving for sublimity is set aside, the sublime breathes forth in the stops of the voices. Conscious sublimity stuffs up the chest. True sublimity opens the nose and chest and we rise as from the deathbed of a cold, giddy with breath.

I too write with the inner ear, listening for feelings. I write no note cards, no outlines, work up no crutches. I trust feelings, not facts. All my writing must come breathing out of me. In *Painted Paragraphs* I pass myself off as an expert on writing, since I think daily about writing, and my largest hardship is to get past facts into feelings and to stir you as I am stirred by the joy of finding my soul alive in other people and my refreshment in the works of fellow writers. The trick is never to write an unfelt word. I wake the dead. I start each work from a dead stillness that quickly becomes an earthquake. You too start my works from a dead stop. I must at once grip you and promise ever more stirring feelings as we go along. My inner ear listens to a voice within trying to wake me up. If I wake up, so will you. If we're both awake, we're in bliss and bound together in a religion stronger than words.

126

What religion? The religion that lifts the Congo like a great white sultry snake into Conrad's mind, a thing writhing free of Victorian rhetoric, the germ in Plutarch that lifts Shakespeare by his spine above a barge on the Nile, the plasm that embodies Wideman in a huge fat tree trunk, or that staggers Stone with the foliate iris of a dead girl in a freezer, or becomes the large few stars of Whitman's blue-tinged summer night. What is this religion that draws us in? Breath! As D. H. Lawrence says "Not I, but the wind that blows through me!" Or as I say about Walt, "Hey, he's not dead, I see his ribs heaving."

A mazy art, this writing, a stir of feelings, the original moil of passions driving to mate writer with reader to become one in a charged state neither can name because each makes up only half of this new passion while each remains a mystery to the other. Whitman: "—the words of my book nothing, the drift everything." All this I love, blowing life into words is black-berries and well-water.

All right, why did I just write that passage? Because I'm looking for the passional languages behind description, pas-sions lighting the untellable places behind landscape. Once I find what I want to describe and the first draft is down, the biggest job is to throw the rubbish out so the reader can hear with my inner ear. Without that clear tie, that static-free chan-nel between us, it's fruitless for me to suggest any larger goal. My spiritual goal is to grant you my life, empower you with my feelings, let you drink from my soul and have that tie wake us both from the dead, forever. I tell you this because that's what every writer in this book is doing: binding his soul to yours.

Take Hemingway. In his middle thirties he made a hunting

trip to Africa and tried to write about it "well and truly" in *Green Hills of Africa*. Returning to Key West after his safari, he begins writing his African journal but decides midway to give the reader a rest from all the hunting and tell about the Gulf Stream outside Havana. He couches this description in a huge paragraph that defends his absenting himself from the social problems of the day and surrendering himself to writing well and truly about things he knows are real, even though his critics say he's faking. But he knows "absolutely" the value of what he writes. His is a "serious occupation," beyond fashion, and when he's alone writing (listening with his inner ear) it's like being alone on the sea, outside Havana on the Gulf Stream, and knowing that the Gulf Stream is something lasting; it moves as it has since before man and it has gone by the shoreline of Cuba since long before Columbus first sighted it, and the things he's found out about it are of lasting value because

that stream will flow, as it has flowed, after the Indians, after the Spaniards, after the British, after the Americans and after all the Cubans and all the systems of governments, the richness, the poverty, the martyrdom, the sacrifice and the venality and the cruelty are all gone as the high-piled scow of garbage, bright-colored, white-flecked, ill-smelling, now tilted on its side, spills off its load into the blue water, turning it a pale green to a depth of four or five fathoms as the load spreads across the surface, the sinkable part going down and the flotsam of palm fronds, corks, bottles, and used electric light globes, seasoned with an occasional condom or a deep floating corset, the torn leaves of a student's exercise book, a well-inflated dog, the occasional rat, the no-longer-distinguished cat; all this well shepherded by the boats of the garbage pickers who pluck their prizes with long poles, as interested, as intelligent, and as accurate as historians; they have the viewpoint; the stream, with no visible flow, takes five loads of this a day when things are going well in La Habana and in ten miles along the coast it is as clear and blue and unimpressed as it was ever before the tug hauled out the scow; and the palm fronds of our victories, the worn light bulbs of our discoveries and the empty condoms of our great loves float with no significance against one single, lasting thing—the stream.

—*Green Hills of Africa* (1935), Ernest Hemingway

This bowled me over in my twenties. Hemingway rarely uses metaphor or simile and when the strong likenesses at the end struck my eye—"the palm fronds of our victories, the worn light bulbs of our discoveries and the empty condoms of our great loves"—my youthful graveyard feelings lighted up admiringly. My feelings came from my age, from the aftermath of World War II and the A-bomb nightmare, the fresh newsreel horrors about the murder of six million Jews, the unbelievable death toll in Russia, God knows what else, and an early darkening brought on by booze. I was a setup for Hemingway's black thoughts.

He writes with great freshness and feeling here. Typing it up I find it sloppy but wonder whether the sideways slide from subject to subject isn't all for the best. Would more full stops make it stronger? Or would they point up weak thoughts? Both. It could open more strongly. His slam at critics who are paid to say his absolutely valuable subjects are fakes is a body blow to a scarecrow. The whole paragraph could stand up better, while the opening statements (which I boil down) fail to disarm us for the big statements ahead. What does work is the long meandering sentence likening itself to the Gulf Stream. This sentence, loaded with tasty nuts and raisins, shows masterly detail though clearer logic would hit harder. I'd rewrite a few phrases: "a gas-filled dog, the passing rat, the fish-eaten cat" for the "well-inflated dog, the occasional rat, the no-longer-distinguished cat." He means, I think, distinguishable—though as a cat fancier he may see all cats as cats of distinction.

The big test is do the many phrases always tie together clearly or must we stop and untangle them? Should we simply surrender to the helter-skelter flow, with its brilliant artistry, or do we ask it to be absolutely valuable, clear at each moment? Even before my quotation above begins, the big paragraph trips over its ankles while lunging onward, so much so that in what I do quote the grammar melts before the flow of feeling. But it's a striking paragraph, and once read it's remembered forever and returned to with relish.

So what do I think about the fatalism of the palm fronds, worn light bulbs and empty condoms? First I weigh them against Hemingway's age, his lifelong tie with death, the beasts he hunted and killed and dead men he saw as a reporter and as a Red Cross ambulance driver and deliverer of cigarettes and snacks on the Italian front in World War I (where he picked up over two hundred pieces of shrapnel and lost a testicle), his father's suicide, the darkness of mind he tells us about in "Big Two-Hearted River," and the nice supply of booze he had along on safari and back home in Cuba. He's a shade younger than Shakespeare when he wrote his graveyard masterpiece *Hamlet*.

What happens when I set Hemingway's blackness beside Whitman's "dead, dead, dead" in "The City Dead-House" which finds divinity not absent in his ruined dead whore? Well, Hemingway's willing to go with his stiff-lipped melancholy and spell it out against a bright Gulf Stream canvas. I like him to go with dark thoughts, experience them. How else work his way through them? By denial? He never *did* work his way through. Instead, he sucked on them until—set ablaze by mental illness—they killed him. So, I admire his art but fight off his feelings.

Okay, his futility aria is foggy. But fog is the best way to get across the weak-minded pessimism he's selling. This is still a great paragraph; it dares, it sings, it works though it breaks the rules, but its romance darkens good sense and leads astray clear thinking. *Poof!* Picasso tells Ernest and slaps his shoulder. *Let the cretins piss on their shoes.*

Fifteen years later, in *The Old Man and the Sea,* Hemingway again went out on the Gulf Stream and with even greater art left his hero defeated but unbroken. Again, this short novel's last scene misfires—its irony focuses on two tourists making dumb remarks about a great marlin spine floating in the harbor, which they mistake for a shark's but which we know is the hero's and Hemingway's spine, not just the marlin's. Their waiter, Hemingway's stand-in, wants to set them straight— but the hero's noble deed remains unsung to these twits. I always sense a falling off of inspiration in ironic climaxes. The indifference of nature or society to human works does not end a story greatly. Great stories defeat irony. You can tell me in noble verse that the paths of glory lead but to the grave—but you can't make me swallow it.

Here's the Gulf Stream without garbage:

They spread apart after they were out of the mouth of the harbor and each one headed for the part of the ocean where he hoped to find fish. The old man knew he was going far out and he left the smell of the land behind and rowed out into the clean early morning smell of the ocean. He saw the phosphorescence of the Gulf weed in the water as he rowed over the part of the ocean that the fishermen called the great well because there was a sudden deep of seven hundred fathoms where all sorts of fish congregated because of the swirl the current made against the steep walls of the floor of the ocean. Here there were concentrations of shrimp and bait fish and sometimes schools of squid in the deepest holes and these rose close to the surface at night where all the wandering fish fed on them. . . .

Before it was really light he had his baits out and was drifting with the current. One bait was down forty fathoms. The second was at seventy-five and the third and fourth were down in the blue water at one hundred and one hundred and twenty-five fathoms. Each bait hung head down with the shank of the hook inside the bait fish, tied and sewed solid and all the projecting part of the hook, the curve and the point, was covered with fresh sardines. Each sardine was hooked through both eyes so that they made a half-garland on the projecting steel. There was no part of the hook that a great fish could feel which was not sweet smelling and good tasting.

—*The Old Man and the Sea* (1952),
Ernest Hemingway

Here's descriptive writing at its most artful and I have no fight with even a word of it. We sense with our whole being the predawn stillness as Santiago rows out of the harbor, we smell the land left behind and the clean early morning smell of the ocean. We glow with the phosphorescence of the Gulf weed. We sink into the abyssal great well. We are one with shrimp and squiggling squid that rise close to the surface at night and are fed on.

Well, Don, why do you accept phosphorescence rather than glow of the Gulf weed? For the same reason I accept Macbeth's guilty hand that will "the multitudinous seas incarnadine, making the green one red"—or the green sea turn red with running blood: phosphorescence imitates the stretch and roll of dark waves full of glowing weed; and multitudinous seas incarnadine [a verb here] imitates Macbeth's hand turning great stretching seas blood-red. *Sometimes* an effect comes off best with Greek or Latin roots.

The second paragraph, with one bait drifting at forty fathoms, one at seventy-five and a third and fourth "down in the blue water at one hundred and one hundred and twenty-five fathoms," is from writers' heaven. When Hemingway tells how the baited hooks are sweet smelling and good tasting, we want to bite right into those sardines—though he's warned us of "the curve and the point" of the hook. I must say I can't tell how the sardines can be hooked through the eyes and yet hang head down. If it's the other bait fish that hang head down, they have to have been hooked from vent to mouth and drawn up the shank of the hook so that each hangs head down, tied and sewed solid, facing a garland of sardines on the curve and point. I see Hemingway's dirty look at me that is sour-smelling and tastes bad as if from a long-uncleaned refrigerator whose power has been off all fall, winter, and spring and whose box of baking soda is now rock-hard and cannot drink up the bad smells or sweeten the sour vegetable bins, and that tells me my thoughts are as webs in his sink and my short-legged words as dead flies on his sill.

I said earlier that death scenes are a writer's banquet, joys we await and gather strength for in our sleep. The trick is to keep calm and try not to cram everything we know about death into one scene. Many grisly details can be ignored and death upgraded so that writer and reader sit back exalted. Harry Morgan's death in Hemingway's *To Have and Have Not*—"No matter how a man alone ain't got no bloody fucking chance"— for me falls short. Remember too that a man or woman who freezes to death in a blizzard or dies alone on a desert is no good to us without a reaction shot, a second person in whom we show our feelings about the dead. We need someone to say, "Good night, sweet prince, may flights of angels sing thee to thy rest"—which I would think speaks Shakespeare's feelings as well as Horatio's and an audience's which has come to like and even love deep-thinking, gifted, not-so-mad Prince Hamlet. Tolstoy lifts heaven and earth to raise our feelings for Ivan Ilych in *The Death of Ivan Ilych,* but the only feeling we have is of amazement as this petty man finds a great spiritual light invading his last seconds of awareness. Ivan Ilych seems unworthy of such unspeakable light, but even he is granted God's peace by Tolstoy, which is the story. A tremendous moment, and a superb turn for the climax. But I'm no longer uplifted in *Ivan Ilych* by anything but Tolstoy's skill and moral purpose, or genius. The reaction shot of Ilych's wife's streaming tears and his son's kissing his hand are replaced by a reaction shot Tolstoy places squarely in the reader—which is more or less of Tolstoy's unseen hand bestowing whatever on this wretch—and this reader isn't moved. I was at twenty-one. But not now.

Back to Egypt! I've been saving till now my favorite descriptive passage by an American novelist. It's about a dead man, an Egyptian, who died about three thousand years ago, has been mummified and awaits rebirth. There's no reaction shot except a passing visit by his mother—Norman Mailer is not trying to move us about his dead hero. After all, we've just met Menenhetet and are setting out on a very long trip with him during which he's reborn as a child through whose eyes much of the novel is told. Menenhetet tells us how he was mummified— every step of it!—and Mailer finds himself in full flower intellectually and in control of songlike words, with every syllable weighed and metaphor measured as never before in his writing.

Menenhetet tells how two embalmers plunge a hook into his brain and through his nose pull out dead flesh in gobbets, then dissolve with lime and ash whatever might be stuck to the inside of his skull. It's a mystery to him how he can go on thinking with no brain, but he feels himself being held upside down with the caustic washing out his eyes. Then the embalmers cut open his belly and empty out his organs and spread them about him in canopic jars. He feels the village of his organs float there in fluids and spices. These scattered parts keep a sense of family—his lungs, liver, stomach and guts remember him. But how different his life had seemed to his liver and his heart! He feels emptier than the belly of a woman who has just given birth as the empty cavity of his body

was now washed, soothed and stimulated, cleansed, peppered, herbified, and left with a resonance through which no hint of the body's corruption could breathe. They scoured the bloody inside with palm wine, and left the memories of

135

my flesh in ferment. They pounded in spices and peppers, and rare sage from the limestone foundations to the West; then came leaves of thyme and the honey of bees who had fed on thyme, the oil of orange was rubbed into the cavity of the ribs, and the oil of lemon balmed the inside of my lower back to free it of the stubborn redolence of the viscera. Cedar chips, essence of jasmine, and branchlets of myrrh were crushed—I could hear the cries of the plants being broken more clearly than the sound of human voices. The myrrh even made its clarion call. A powerful aromatic (as powerful in the kingdom of herbs as the Pharaoh's voice) was the myrrh laid into the open shell of my body. Next came cinnamon leaves, stem, and cinnamon bark to sweeten the myrrh. Like rare powders added to the sweetmeats in the stuffing of a pigeon, were these bewildering atmospheres they laid into me. . . .

Cleaned, stuffed, and trussed, I was deposited in a bath of natron—that salt which dries the meat to stone—and there I lay with weights to keep me down. . . . Like a stone washed by fog, baked by sun, and given the flavor of the water on the bank, I was entering that universe of the dumb where it was part of our gift to hear the story told by every wind to every stone.

—*Ancient Evenings* (1983), Norman Mailer

Why does this strike me so deeply? Well, it's grown-up stuff that kindles my child's sense of fantasy, as if a forensic pathologist were studying astral travel in the bones of Flash Gordon. It takes a mad dream seriously and makes it concrete. Even the voice enthralls me. I'm all for any writer who can tell me about his village of jarred guts and organs still existing about him.

Fearless imagination as huge-fingered as a Mahler adagio calls down the stars. Mailer's long, amazingly sensuous set piece about mummification appeals to my heart's core.

What works about this voice? First, it's modest. It begins forcefully with a hook that batters and plunges into the story-teller's brain and brings out "pieces, gobbets, and whole parts of the dead flesh of my mind . . ." then becomes softer, once we're hooked, fixing us into an unbelievable event with great bodily presence.

Menenhetet clearly admires the skill of his mummy makers. Just as his voice sucks us headily into the spices and herbs being pounded into his empty hollows, his wonder washes over us as he lies weighted in the salt bath for three days hardening into stone. The storyteller becomes a big seashell, hears an ocean roaring in his ears as old voices pass across the sands, the ocean *is* sand, and he enters "that universe of the dumb where it was part of our gift to hear the story told by every wind to every stone."

Mailer promised for thirty years to write a novel like this, one whose power of imagination would knock America on its ass. The irony is that his story should take place three thousand years ago in Egypt. He had to be plucked out of America to loosen all restraints on his imagination. How much of the passage above comes from research? Probably all of it. Does it read "worked up"? Not for a moment, any more than Shakespeare's lightning rewrite of Plutarch smells of midnight oil in the gorgeousness of *Antony and Cleopatra.* Who cares where it came from? All dross is smelted away and the gold lumps beaten into sheets. Anything I'd rewrite? Not a breath of it. To my joy, Mailer loads *Ancient Evenings* with brilliancies everywhere—and not a stuffed bird among them. Don't miss the boy Menenhetet's shimmering boat journey into Memphi, its big painted paragraphs noisy with life and as triumphant as any in Melville. In them, just as Menenhetet earlier told us about his organs being a village, so Memphi is a village in Mailer, as is ancient Egypt, a gigantic golden circuitry of imagination; he lays out all the organs of the city for us to feast on as we listen to lives relived in melting blue afternoons and the turquoise twilight of Egyptian evenings.

I've not spoken of moral force in description for some pages; no need to spell it out time and again. My final excerpts ring with moral force, if I may say that when including pages from my own work.

Tolstoy's "Strider—The Story of a Horse" is as moral as fiction gets while still holding the power to shake our spines. Strider is a piebald—a white horse with three huge black spots on the head and neck, side, and hindquarters. Because of his coloring, he's thought strange, even by other horses. One chestnut filly though befriends him when they're young. Strider's now old and teased by merciless young fillies in his corral. One night, after the other horses have kicked and beaten him, Strider tells them his story, in horse language. He tells of his happy youth, then of the day he was gelded and how his life changed forever. All joy leaked out of him. He was sold and passed through many hands. Prince Serpukhovskoy, a spendthrift racing through two million rubles, bought him and won several races with Strider pulling a sulky. Then Strider was whipped through a brutal sixteen-mile run by the stupid prince and never regained his wind. Though the prince sold him, Strider recalls him fondly. Ten years later the bankrupt prince is flabby, aged, soaked with brandy and cigar smoke, and lives off his mistress.

One night Strider is taken out by Vaska, the peasant, who gets drunk and lets Strider stand all night outside a tavern. After Strider and a peasant horse lick each other throughout the night, Strider comes down with mange mites. In the morning he returns to the herd but keeps rubbing himself. Five days pass, the vet comes and tells Vaska that Strider has the itch. Vaska sends for the knacker and tells him to cut Strider's throat.

Behind the barn the knacker whets his knife. Strider sighs to the sound of the sharpening of the knife and his hanging lower lip shows his worn yellow teeth. Suddenly his head is lifted. Two dogs wait, sniffing at the knacker, and watch Strider. Then his throat hurts. He shudders, kicks with one foot, but holds back to see what's next. Maybe he's being doctored, he thinks. But something streams down his neck and chest. Now he sighs profoundly, feeling much better. "The whole burden of his life was eased." His legs quiver, he sways, surprised, starts forward, but his legs entangle, he falls.

When Strider's convulsions cease, the knacker turns him on his back and skins him. This part of the story, of course, is not told by Strider.

That evening the herd returns and down below sees something red, with the dogs busy at it and hawks and crows overhead. The peasants can hardly drive away the chestnut filly.

At dawn, a lean old wolf comes out of the forest and into a glade and begins feeding her joyfully howling five big-headed cubs. Her belly's so full her dugs drag. The cubs circle her as she turns to the smallest and holding her muzzle down convulses, opening her large sharp-toothed jaws, and heaves up a large piece of horseflesh.

The bigger cubs rushed towards her, but she moved threateningly at them and let the little one have it all. The little one, growling as if in anger, pulled the horseflesh under him and began to gorge. In the same way the mother wolf coughed up a piece for the second, the third, and all five of them, and then lay down in front of them to rest.

A week later only a large skull and two shoulder-blades lay behind the barn; the rest had all been taken away. In summer a peasant, collecting bones, carried away these shoulder-blades and skull and put them to use.

The dead body of Serpukhovskoy, which had walked about the earth eating and drinking, was put under ground much later. Neither his skin, nor his flesh, nor his bones, were of any use.

Just as for the last twenty years his body that had walked the earth had been a great burden to everybody, so the putting away of that body was again an additional trouble to people. He had not been wanted by anybody for a long time and had only been a burden, yet the dead who bury their dead found it necessary to clothe that swollen body, which at once began to decompose, in a good uniform and good boots and put it into a new and expensive coffin with new tassels at its four corners, and then to take it to Moscow and there dig up some long buried human bones, and to hide in that particular spot this decomposing maggotty body in its new uniform and polished boots, and cover it all up with earth.

—"Strider—The Story of a Horse" (1865)
The Portable Tolstoy, edited by John Bayley,
translated by Louise and Aylmer Maude

How's that for unsentimental? Tolstoy was about thirty-five when he wrote "Strider." Readers were struck dumb not just by the moral but also by Tolstoy's power to render the thoughts of animals, a power he put to use many times. Anyone who has the genius to read the minds of animals is someone to listen to. He published as well the first volumes of *War and Peace* at this time, which also shocked readers with its psychological realism and quickly placed him as Russia's greatest living writer. No writer has since gripped the whole world with his mastery to the same degree as Tolstoy. I too was gripped by him and when young read the entire twenty-two volumes of his complete works in the Oxford World Classics edition of hand-sized blue books printed on India paper. If you wonder why I go on about moral force, that's the reason, thousands upon thousands of thin, delicate leaves of my hard-staring, blue-eyed master. Today I feel no need to reread his novels, though his light-bringing psychological and later spiritual artistry still gives me pleasure. His message is in my marrow. I could never be a lapsed Tolstoyan.

Without warning Tolstoy leads us into the horse's death: Strider laps a horse we don't know is sick. Lonely horses, tethered all night at a tavern door, they comfort each other. And how fast the mites strike—the very next morning the itch begins. Earlier in the story, during a glossed-over gelding scene, we don't even know Strider is being castrated. The gelder's knife is as sharp as the knacker's; we're told only, by Strider, "I ceased neighing for ever. All my energy died away."

This must be the first semi–stream-of-consciousness story told by a horse, a daring idea in 1865. Most writers could flesh out such a story with three or four things they know about horses. Tolstoy, going right into the horse's mind, stays there like God for most of the story. Strider's death comes to him finely—he doesn't even know his throat's cut or he's bleeding or what the devilish two dogs are waiting for—they've seen this before and know the knacker's bloodstained coat. Then Strider senses something: "The whole burden of his life was eased." Ah, the Russian readers cried, What genius! And I joined them. But Strider's not dead yet: "Everything was so new to him." How does Tolstoy know that? We don't care, we're just amazed at its rightness. Actually, huge mood changes and sudden world-clearness are a commonplace of Russian writing, states called estrangement and defamiliarization, something like the letting go before an epileptic attack: characters in Tolstoy and Dostoyevski suddenly stand outside themselves and see life in a new light whose freshness and strength estrange them from their old lives. Here Tolstoy grants estrangement to Strider (since he himself is Strider). When he first began doing this, the device was so original that his readers went into ecstatic fits: "Somebody else has felt this strange!" I too felt it, though a century later.

The knacker rolls Strider over, four legs up, and skins his mangy hide: that doesn't happen to many horses in fiction, nor does getting his bones cracked by dogs when he's only "something red." And a few hours later comes the first reaction shot, with the chestnut filly, Strider's old friend, watching dogs tear meat loose: "The chestnut filly stopped, stretched out her head and neck, and sniffed the air for a long time. They could hardly drive her away."

Ahhh! Note the restraint, no Hollywood madness of roping the crazed filly—only a madness implied, with Tolstoy expressing pity. Mild pity, because the horror of Strider's death has been underplayed: despite the mental shock of each detail, the full horror is not stated, the more grisly side—how the upside-down horse's cut throat looked, the blood in the gray hairs of his belly, his gelded parts—is veiled. Would they have added to the horror, given us a deeper pity? Maybe. But this is not the tragedy of a horse, it's a moral tale. Tolstoy/Strider is still alive, after all, writing this. Pity would sentimentalize.

And then the mother wolf, whom Tolstoy seems to have slept with. Her leanness and shedding coat, her loaded belly scraping her dugs along the ground, her bending down on one knee to feed the oddest cub first—what doesn't he know about her? It's not easy to get that close to a wolf bitch to find these things out. I hear Turgenev shout at his mistress, "How did Lev Nikolayevich know that! Is he *God*?" Many thought Tolstoy's gifts sheer miracle.

The last two paragraphs make up the only ironic climax that ever moved me, with the burial of Serpukhovskoy's useless corpse set beside Strider being fed to the dogs and wolves and hawks and crows. Tolstoy goes for the maggots now, he vilifies. He falls on Serpukhovskoy like a manhole cover and sets the dead man's ears ringing. He invents graveyard environmentalism—a new school? He cuts the throat of all our received ideas about death and leaves all rivals agape.

Has he a real point or is he just a bloody snot? What if Serpukhovskoy had been a wonderful guy, beloved, and given his two million rubles to charity: he'd still be buried with the same honors and the same maggots. Is setting his foul burial beside Strider's dog and wolf meat a false excuse for moralizing?

I'll get back to Tolstoy. Nadezhda Mandelstam (1889–1980) was the wife of the great, buoyant Russian poet Osip Mandelstam (1891–1938), a nonreligious Jew. Her memoir *Hope Against Hope* (1970) for the most part is about his last four years, between his first arrest in 1934, for a ripely stinking poem about Stalin, and his and Nadezhda's exile in the Urals, his next arrest and his ghastly death while waiting shipment to a work camp. Her second memoir, *Hope Abandoned* (1972), fills in biographical gaps in *Hope Against Hope* and tells of her painful wanderings after his death and of her work at keeping his banned poetry alive. His name had been sponged out of Soviet literature, and Nadezhda, still exiled, made a bare hand-to-mouth existence by teaching English. She had a doctorate in English philology, and her name in English means hope. It was her English translator who entitled her nameless memoir *Hope Against Hope,* and then she herself insisted the second volume be called *Hope Abandoned.*

Her isolation following Osip's arrest, throughout the war years, and even into the fifties and sixties when she wrote her two memoirs, is unimaginable to a Western mind: a corner in a communal flat, a bed, a bare light bulb—for decades—as we are told by the legendary poet Anna Akhmatova's biographer, Anatoly Nayman, in his memoir *Remembering Anna Akhmatova.* Nayman tells about visiting Nadezhda in Pskov with poet Joseph Brodsky in 1962, and finding her half invalided, on her bed, living in squalor. Following the publication of *Hope Abandoned* in the West in 1972, Nayman took exception to Nadezhda's portrait of Anna Akhmatova, and in his memoir he calls Nadezhda's picture of Anna "a subtle well-measured dose of untruths dissolved in truth and there is no way of removing the malignant matter without damage to the tissues." (Marvelous!) He suggests that Nadezhda, at the time of writing her memoirs, was not in her full mind and tells that she lived in terror of the secret police once the memoirs were finished, copied by others and being read underground. I mention this because Nadezhda's state of mind while writing her memoirs seems to harmonize with the mentality of camp life which she describes below. However, her husband's English translator, Clarence Brown, who knew Nadezhda and also wrote a biography of Osip, *Mandelstam* (1973), speaks of her playing at times the role of "poet's widow," and that ". . . the sweetly sad figure who had dispensed this and that fact of her husband's biography (even glancing at times, in her hammier moments, over her shoulder) would clear the general air with some spine-shattering Russian oath and revert to her true nature: a vinegary, Brechtian, steelhard woman of great intelligence, limitless courage, no illusions, permanent convictions and a wild sense of the absurdity of life."

In the last pages of *Hope Against Hope,* she is visited by Kazarnovski, a journalist/prisoner at the camp to which Osip Mandelstam was to be sent. She hides the disordered journalist from the police for three months and sucks out of him everything he knows about her husband and his death. He had been with Osip in the transit camp where they awaited shipment to the Kolyma work camp. Kazarnovski's memory, she says, "was like a huge, rancid pancake in which fact and fancy from his prison days had been mixed up together and baked into an inseparable mass." She writes:

I already knew that this kind of affliction of the memory was not peculiar to the wretched Kazarnovski or a result of drinking too much vodka. It was a feature of almost all the former camp inmates I have met immediately after their release—they had no memory for dates or the passage of time and it was difficult for them to distinguish between things they had actually experienced themselves and stories they had heard from others. Places, names, events and their sequence were all jumbled up in the minds of these broken people, and it was never possible to disentangle them. Most accounts of life in the camps appeared on first hearing to be a disconnected series of stories about the critical moments when the narrator nearly died but then miraculously managed to save himself. The whole of camp life was reduced to these highlights, which were intended to show that although it was almost impossible to survive, man's will to live was such that he came through nevertheless. Listening to these accounts, I was horrified at the thought that there might be nobody who could ever properly bear witness to the past. Whether inside or outside the camps, we had all lost our memories. But it later turned out that there were people who had made it their aim from the beginning not only to save themselves, but to survive as witnesses. These relentless keepers of the truth, merging with all the other prisoners, had bided their time—there were probably more such people in the camps than outside, where it was all too common to succumb to the temptation to make terms with reality and live out one's life in peace. Of course those witnesses who have kept a clear memory of the past are few in number, but their very survival is the best proof that good, not evil, will prevail in the end.

—*Hope Against Hope* (1970), Nadezhda Mandelstam,
translated by Max Hayward

A page later she writes that sometimes, in his calmer moments, the birdlike, "endlessly life-glad" Mandelstam recited poetry to his fellow prisoners, "and some of them may even have made copies. I have seen 'albums' with his verse which circulated in the camps. Once he was told by somebody that in one of the death cells in Lefortovo a line from one of his poems had been scratched on the wall: 'Am I real and will death really come?' When he heard this, M. cheered up and was much calmer for a few days."

Heartbreaking.

A leader murders millions upon millions of his countrymen, and beheads the intelligentsia first of all, creating a society mad down to its roots. There's no place to hide. Mandelstam's "endlessly life-glad" spirit could not live in such blackness. He gags at Stalin's prescription for correct writing, grows contemptuous of paper and ink, writes his poems in his head and keeps them "entire in the interior dark." He is *not* a writer. "I have no manuscripts, no notebooks, no archives. I have no handwriting because I never write. I alone in Russia work from the voice while all around me the bitch-pack writes. What the hell kind of writer am I!? Get out you fools!" Signing his own death warrant was the only possible way to live as a free man and remain gay on the lip of the abyss. After long horror, he said in 1937, the year before he died, "I do not repudiate either the living or the dead."

In reading Nadezhda we cannot part her from the spirit of Mandelstam—whom Vladimir Nabokov called "poor, marvelous Mandelstam." What makes her passages from *Hope Against Hope* so rending? Well, first, our amazement that anyone could even write what she wrote amid the roiling darkness of mid-century Soviet life. Hers is not an untrustworthy report from a biased Western news agency. This is a voice burning like a laser through the monstrous cancer of communism, a political system that morally paralyzed its citizenry with an internal spy apparatus of infinite complexity and resourcefulness—a system whereunder, Nadezhda says, "human blood is like water." We get a first hint of this when she likens Kazarnovski to a rancid pancake, "his prison days . . . mixed up together and baked into an inseparable mass," and we sense the delirium and blurring of gray camp life behind barbed wire where, she tells us later, "the dead with numbered tags on their legs lay side by side with the living . . . I can be certain of only one thing: that somewhere M.'s sufferings ended in death. Before his death, he must have lain dying on his bunk like others around him."

The passage has the immediacy of being struck off all at once by someone who did not have the luxury of revision and yet it works artfully toward a mind-reeling turn or emotional enlargement. First we are told what we already think we know about camp life, though she goes more deeply into the melting down of memory than we expect. Then she withdraws surprisingly, taking a larger view, and says, "Listening to these accounts, I was horrified at the thought that there might be nobody who could ever properly bear witness to the past. Whether inside or outside the camps, we had all lost our memories." A whole people—rememoried! This shocks, and for me is the paragraph's great pivot, although she works out her idea still more keenly, saying that even those prisoners determined to remember the facts would "succumb to the temptation to make terms with reality and live out one's life in peace." And yet some few, very few, like Aleksandr Solzhenitsyn, did keep memory intact—although Solzhenitsyn's novels cover the forced-labor camps of 1945 to 1953, not the death traps of the

Great Purge and war years. Do we believe her little Latin moral at the end, that the survival of Solzhenitsyn and some few others "is the best proof that good, not evil, will prevail in the end"? Is this any less sentimental than Madame de Sévigné's letter to her daughter? Well, yes, it is. The existence of Solzhenitsyn's novels seemingly does prove that truth will slay falsehood. Though his novels bear witness as works of art, not as memoirs, and as history are doubtless as mixed up as Kazarnovski's memories, it may well be that fancy orders facts more truthfully than photographic reminiscences. Nadezhda herself shuffles chronology and reorders facts to achieve greater moral force. We come away from *Hope Against Hope* enriched by a description of the breaking fibers of a nation's mind as a madman's paranoia dissolves downward into the bowels of his people, and by our touching a poet whose works have already outlasted his murderer's monuments. Even dead, he writes on, in the back rooms of his eyes. I hear Stalin muttering in hell, "That little assassin!"

My lift for the following passage from my autobiography came from a desire to write in sobriety as wildly and freely as I thought I wrote when drinking. I'd long thought drink unlocked ecstasy. It did, but the writing was gorgeous slush. Sober I found an ecstasy other than the befogged heaven of alcohol. *This* clearheaded ecstasy was much like Tolstoy's when he arrived at the deaths of Strider and Serpukhovskoy and felt beside himself with lip-curling joy as word after word nailed down the theme he'd been working out from the story's first word.* My

---

*It took him twenty years to write; he'd begun it simply to show the thoughts of a horse, then hit the snag of nowhere to go; some years after a vast estrangement from himself, and having taken up a cudgel for the Kingdom of Heaven,

idea when drinking, and later, was that the reader must be kept riveted to a cloud. Beside himself, his feet off the earth. Do most novelists have this goal—or do they jog once more around a worn footpath? Me, I want to float over the page and squeeze feelings down on the reader every moment—keep him half drunk. Storytelling is feelings, feelings, feelings. Thousands of books tell how to write, but not one how to feel, how to turn ink into live nerve matter and light up your reader's spine. No finger on feelings, only a thousand on craft. Hey, I'm just being personal. But how do you think Tolstoy felt when he stepped into his story and looking down from Olympus sniffed at "the dead who bury their dead . . ."? Why does Tolstoy set up a straw man like Serpukhovskoy to piss all over? You don't know? Sure you do—by now in this book you must. Tolstoy *is* Serpukhovskoy, just as I am that craft-ridden critic I keep beating up. And he's the horse who gave Strider the mange. Tolstoy is pissing on his own past as a spendthrift cavalry officer, seducer of peasant girls, father of bastards, glutton for whores, heavy smoker and drinker, and idiot gambling away his inheritance who saved his homestead only by a thread. He is burying the past and pissing on its grave.

And so do I. My excerpt begins with a visit to my mother in Florida:

We got drunk. I fell into a frenzy and beat her. I tore out her phone, busted her lamps and waded into her again—her suckling baby, her schoolboy, her brilliant son the class vice-

---

he returned to Strider and worked in Serpukhovskoy as the foil who would prove his story's moral—whatever that is.

150

president, her military school cadet, her Marine, her college student, her married son, her airman, her son the father, and then her divorced son, her unpublished son, her drinking son the reporter and carwrecker, her whoring son back from Europe, her fat bearded son in Manhattan, and her mother-beating son, heavy legs in bermudas, puffy eyes without pity—trying to slap her into sobriety and salvation. Who was I beating?

For the fifth drunken time in my life, I was thrown into jail. In the morning the jailer came and led me, clubbed and stunned, hair flying, next to naked and barefoot as a shithouse rat, from my cell. We went into an elevator. Utterly silent, it seemed to fall on foam. "What's happening?" I asked. "Your bail's been paid, sonny." I knew he was pulling my Yankee leg. The doors parted open like cobweb. That marvel of a bailer stood before me, not a foot away. She had a black eye.

I was now almost two-hundred-and-fifty pounds, red-faced, losing my hair, given to cankers and bleeding gums, pissing so often I'd use the kitchen sink instead of the toilet, finding my teeth and nails loosening, a victim of boils, my eyes were pink, tired, dry and scratchy and the lids stuck together with mucal infection when I slept, my ears rang and were supersensitive to any scrape or screech, I gave off a staleness no soap could reach, my crotch and privates were forever raw and cracked, I was losing the hair off my shins and pubis, my bellybutton stank and I shaved my armpits to no avail, my nose enlarged and capillaries split, the insides of my ears were raw from flaking, my tastebuds wore smooth at the rear and grew apart up front so that I oversalted everything and could awaken before breakfast only with a tablespoon of salty redhot pepper sauce, my skin eroded in the creases and rubbed off in balls, I had a relentless belch for years from an ulcer, a liver that was trying to get out of me and die somewhere, lastingly stained shitty shorts and wine gas that ate holes in them, breath that even I couldn't stand, sweaty cold soles and shoes I hid in a closet or on the fire-escape if I had a girl overnight, I gasped during any kind of work and could not get a full breath even while typing, I began waking up nightly on the floor having convulsed out of my bed, wine trots were common and many hours spent near tears trying to wring out my bowels on the toilet, my pulse seemed to clog and dribble, I had false angina in my upper left chest regularly, someone was going to shoot me in my rocker so I moved it away from the window, but I had a waking dream for ten years of my brain exploding on im-pact, I would lie unable to wake up but not asleep while strange men moved about my kitchen and livingroom (they weren't there), I could not sit comfortably in any position, I smelled of stale semen between my weekly or biweekly baths, my gut bubbled day and night and I'd try to overfeed it to sleep, I had a two-year sinus cold and special flue attacks that laid me out near death, I was hoarse and kept grenadine and lime syrups and pastilles for my hack, my memory self-destructed on the phone and I'd hang up wondering whom I'd talked with or what arrangements we'd made, I often cried out "I'm coming!" when no one had knocked and I answered or heard the phone ring when it was long gone for nonpayment, I felt fungoid and sexually impotent for two years, I slept poorly and kept a pot by my bed in case I couldn't make the sink, I heard people laughing while I was trying to read and metallic sounds that echoed, my overswollen brain rolled liquidly in my skull, I got dizzy rising from chairs or picking up a handful of spilled coins, must I mention mere headaches and hangovers, my bloody morning shaves with safety razors, the mental fog that had me leaning on the table trying to remember my middle name, my age or where I just laid down my glasses, my rage over a dropped spoon or lost paper lying before me on my desk or the endless drinking glasses snapping to pieces in the sink, my poor handling of kitchen knives, and the strange yellow bruises that wandered up and down my arms and biceps, my harsh nerves and weird fugue states on paralyzingly gruesome images of loved people, the living dead people standing around my bed for hours on end (they're worth two mentions), and just normal things everybody had like wanting to sob all the time, especially over the sunset beaches and bathers in the vodka ads, divorced wife and kid, any lost piece of cake or life or unearned joy as a pretext for just letting go with a thirty-minute screamer on the couch, and such clinical loneliness that my cat talked to me. When this happened one morning I thought I'd had a break-through on the language of animals and couldn't wait to test my powers on a dog. Loneliness? I sprayed my icebox fire-truck red and pasted it solid with a collage of breasts. When I filled it tight with big green sweating quarts I'd embrace it in a sex act. I had eleven cats and kittens and they all died in a two-week plague. I tried to hammer the last suffering big one to death on the roof ledge but its head was solid bone and so I threw it still alive six flights down into an empty lot where it turned with a broken back until dead. Music corkscrewed from my bedroom wall. Until my middle thirties I'd detested fantasy and lying to myself, then one night I gave in and was lost, allowing myself any sweet dream under my roving finger palps. During better times I took two hundred acid trips, stocked hash, grass, speed, pey-ote, psilocybin, and kept a moon of opium like ground figs

153

in my icebox. Barren of drugs, I'd grind up morning-glory seeds from the hardware store, down them hulls and all with wine—they were hallucinogenic in those days (no longer)—then sit for hours in nightwinds under a hard bright moon and watch blue clouds unshadow Tompkins Square Park, loony as a June poet. And much, much more. I was a universe of unrecognized symptoms, fighting down wine, throwing up through my nose, fighting down more and thinking I was happy. Why go on? Let's get to my real life—although I don't deny I had some time in heaven as a drunk, even after the booze got to me, which was fairly early, fifteen or so, or maybe I should date it from my under-the-bridge blackout with my hometown Marine buddy in Asheville. It doesn't matter. I denied it all the way.

—*Those Drinking Days: Myself and
Other Writers* (1981), Donald Newlove

There was no single day when all of those disasters happened at once; the passage is a roundup. The mother I was beating was the same one I saw at five, "the face of love and I see her now at the great round mirror of her vanity, tracing lines on her plucked brows and deepening the starlight of her youth, my movie beauty . . ." Aside from the joy I had finding the exact word for each symptom, grouping the symptoms by kind, and tuning up rhythms so that no part was overworked or series of parts swollen, the larger use of this black dirge is to sink the reader so deep into the raw red glans of my pain that when I arrive at recovery, recovery sends him or her on a cannonball out of hell. Recovery wasn't that quick but the trip into heaven leaves the reader with this message:

Getting unpickled meant recovering my life from the fog and looking at it. I didn't believe I'd been so bad, possibly I wasn't even a drunk. Or clinical alcoholic. Just a heavy drinker pulling back before deep illness gripped me. Plenty of hope, look how easy it's been. Just focus on good food, vitamins, cut down on salt, sweets, caffeine. What's so hard about feeling good, with sleep and a fulfilling sex life. . . . The lifegiving lift of taking alcohol out of my body, that alone was the main work to be done, as was shown by my superhuman energies, tireless head for reviewing, vigor for order and sharp edge to my eye and sensations. Harps rippled, health bubbled in, I went into superlight—a shining blindness of pink clouds and romantic overload. I felt "powerful, fearless, surprising," as Kafka says of the writer when his spirit is moving. A man who sheds a chemical manhole cover he's been humping for twenty years can't help wanting to bound over light bills, the rent and bourgeois piffle. True life is real magic—spinach and iron!—and Giant Despair lies with his skull cracked in the sunwash. Me sober, I want write.

—*Those Drinking Days: Myself and Other Writers* (1981), Donald Newlove

This passage of seeming recovery leads into five years of slips, so don't think I make recovery a greased shoehorn. During those years of slips and climbing back, I talked to myself a lot, even as I had while drinking ("Me high, I want write!"), but my talk now stemmed from a need to focus on clear goals. And for that I needed clear words. My favorite writer became John Bunyan and my favorite character Mr. Great-Heart from *Pilgrim's Progress*. I'm not a Christian, Jew, Buddhist, Muslim or member of any religion, I'm a recovering drunk with a liquid trapdoor ever behind me. So when I turned to Bunyan, it wasn't for Jesus or Christian uplift—though I have warm feelings about Jesus himself—but for stripped, no-shit words that could break rock and move like steroids into my back muscles. I could get tearful over Bunyan, because what he describes in his novel is the conversion experience, which differs little from getting sober, or passing from chemical despair to a steel bonding with hope.

Here is Christian's awakening to his hopeless state. It starts with Bunyan falling asleep in a cave, the barest kind of dirt hole in the earth, and dreaming—a babe about to be born— no literary dream, this drear mental disorder sucks Bunyan into itself body and soul.

As I walked through the wilderness of this world, I lighted on a certain place where was a Den, and I laid me down in that place to sleep: and as I slept I dreamed a dream. I dreamed, and behold I saw a man clothed with rags, standing in a certain place, with his face from his own house, a book in his hand, and a great burden upon his back. I looked, and saw him open the book and read therein; and as he read, he wept and trembled; and not being able longer to contain, he brake out with a lamentable cry, saying, "What shall I do?"

In this plight, therefore, he went home and refrained himself as long as he could, that his wife and children should not perceive his distress; but he could not be silent long, because that his trouble increased. Wherefore at length he brake his mind to his wife and children; and thus he began to talk to them. O my dear wife, said he, and you the children of my bowels, I, your dear friend, am in myself undone by reason of a burden that lieth hard upon me; moreover, I am for certain informed that this our city will be burned with fire from heaven, in which fearful overthrow both myself, with thee my wife, and you my sweet babes, shall miserably come to ruin, except (the which yet I see not) some way of escape can be found, whereby we may be delivered. At this his relations were sore amazed; not for that they believed that what he had said to them was true, but because they thought that some frenzy distemper had got into his head; therefore, it drawing towards night, and they hoping that sleep might settle his brains, with all haste they got him to bed. But the night was as troublesome to him as the day; wherefore, instead of sleeping, he spent it in sighs and tears. So, when the morning was come, they would know how he did. He told them, Worse and worse: he also set to talking to them again: but they began to be hardened. They also thought to drive away his distemper by harsh and surly behavior to him; sometimes they would deride, sometimes they would chide, and sometimes they would quite neglect him. Wherefore he began to retire himself to this chamber, to pray for and pity them, and also to condole his own misery; he would also walk solitarily in the fields, sometimes reading, and sometimes praying: and thus for some days he spent his time.

Now I saw, upon a time when he was walking in the fields, that he was (as he was wont) reading in his book, and greatly distressed in his mind; and as he read, he burst out, as he had done before, crying, "What shall I do to be saved?"

I saw also that he looked this way and that way, as if he would run; yet he stood still, because (as I perceived) he could not tell which way to go. I looked then, and saw a man named Evangelist coming to him, who asked, Wherefore dost thou cry?

He answered, Sir, I perceive by the book in my hand that I am condemned to die, and after that to come to judgment, and I find that I am not willing to do the first, nor able to do the second.

Then said Evangelist, Why not willing to die, since this life is attended with so many evils? The man answered, Because I fear that this burden that is upon my back will sink me lower than the grave, and I shall fall into Tophet [condemned ground near Jerusalem where children were unlawfully sacrificed to Moloch; now Hell]. And, sir, if I be not fit to go to prison, I am not fit to go to judgment, and from thence to execution; and the thoughts of these things make me cry.

Then said Evangelist, If this be thy condition, why standest thou still? He answered, Because I know not whither to go. Then he gave him a parchment roll, and there was written within, "Fly from the wrath to come."

The man therefore read it, and looking upon Evangelist very carefully, said, Whither must I fly? Then said Evangelist, pointing with his finger over a very wide field, Do you see yonder wicket-gate? The man said, No. Then said the other, Do you see yonder shining light? He said, I think I do. Then said Evangelist, Keep that light in your eye, and go up directly thereto: so shalt thou see the gate; at which when thou knockest it shall be told thee what thou shalt do. So I saw in my dream that the man began to run. Now, he had not run far from his own door, but his wife and children perceiving it, began to cry after him to return; but the man put his fingers in his ears, and ran on, crying, Life! life! eternal life! So he looked not behind him, but fled towards the middle of the plain.

The neighbors also came out to see him run; and as he ran, some mocked, others threatened, and some cried after him to return. . . .

—*Pilgrim's Progress* (1678), John Bunyan

This man is crazed. He will never sleep soundly again until he finds assurance of eternal life. Bunyan instantly draws us into him with simple words showing bizarre actions: "frenzy distemper," "sleep might settle his brains," "he wept and trembled," "he brake out," his family is "sore amazed." And they think he's nuts, jumbled, a hard case. Bunyan sketches in the family with only a few, skillful strokes as the earthbound wife and children first try to calm him and then, as his mind loosens even more, "they began to be hardened." Father is now the family idiot. Fire from heaven? His mind's not right. Bunyan sees his drama as vividly as if on LSD or pot, and not just here but throughout the novel. Even the family so far takes on an aura, as does the field where the man walks alone, reading, trying to pray his way out of his misery. In fact, his brain takes on density and weight, especially in the fearful detail of his plunging his fingers into his ears as he runs off (that's worthy of Goya), tearing himself from the pleas of wife and children, and running across a plain, crying, Life! life! eternal life! with even the neighbors coming out to mock and threaten him. This may be allegory but it spreads through my system like snakebite. I get excited by Bunyan.

For his preaching, Bunyan, who by trade was a mender of tin pots, kettles, pans and what have you, was given twelve years in Bedford prison. In prison he wrote his two greatest books, *Grace Abounding to the Chief of Sinners* (1666), a record of God's deal-

159

ings with him, and *Pilgrim's Progress* (published in 1678, but written earlier). I modeled *Those Drinking Days* on *Grace Abounding,* which is my favorite Bunyan: he goes swearing, drinking and whoring with a charged feverishness that never wearies me. His words strike on bone with no hint of refinement and yet no commonness. He pitches his lines below the King James Bible but higher than shoptalk. What did I say earlier: "True life is real magic—spinach and iron!—and Giant Despair lies with his skull cracked in the sunwash." What was I talking about? Breaking out of a chemical dungeon.

In *Grace Abounding* Bunyan tells how midway through his jail sentence, he was offered freedom if he wouldn't preach. Once out, he couldn't keep silent, and was thrown back in jail to serve five more years. Parting from his wife and children, and his blind child in particular, brought grief. Remember, this is written while still in prison and after many years, as he looks back on the day he came in:

Before I came to prison, I saw what was a-coming, and had especially two considerations warm upon my heart; the first was how to endure, should my imprisonment be long and tedious; the second was how to be able to encounter death, should that be here my portion . . . [He turns to the Bible and finds quotations of great help to him, then decides:] So that I see the best way to go through sufferings is to trust in God through Christ, as touching the world to come; and as touching this world, to count "the grave my house, to make my bed in darkness, and to say to corruption, Thou *art* my father and to the worm, *Thou art* my mother and my sister." That is, to familiarise these things to me.

But not withstanding these helps, I found myself a man,

and compassed with infirmities; the parting with my wife and poor children hath oft been to me in this place as the pulling of flesh from my bones, and that not only because I am somewhat too too fond of those great mercies, but also because I should have often brought to my mind the many hardships, miseries and wants that my poor family was like to meet with, should I be taken from them, especially my poor blind child, who lay nearer my heart than all I had besides; O the thoughts of the hardship I thought my blind one might go under, would break my heart to pieces.

Poor child, thought I, what sorrow art thou like to have for thy portion in this world? Thou must be beaten, must beg, suffer hunger, cold, nakedness, and a thousand calamities, though I cannot now endure the wind should blow upon thee. But yet recalling myself, thought I, I must venture you all with God, though it goeth to the quick to leave you. Oh, I saw in this condition I was as a man who was pulling down his house upon the head of his wife and children; yet thought I, I must do it, I must do it. . . .

—*Grace Abounding to the Chief of Sinners* (1666), John Bunyan

For me this may be the highwatermark of English prose. I can't think of another passage as condensed and moving. Here is real life at its most agonized, but Bunyan writes it straight out, flat, and yet with a power that defies breastbeating and gloom-mongering. And what is he telling us? About the life ahead for his blind child, whom even before he leaves he can't bear the wind to blow on, but who faces a life of blindness in the hard streets of Bedford, and will be beaten as a heretic, must beg, suffer hunger, cold, nakedness, and a thousand calamities—without a father. It is possible to write from strength about the worst calamities in your life.

He has taken his child's blindness within him, he knows his church is under the State's heel, his family's neighbors will mock and threaten, he knows the bitter English winter. As I read things, his own soul is his blind child, and both his child at home and his soul in prison must suffer blindly. Leaving his child at home truly is as he says, "the pulling of flesh from my bones." He means it. This isn't pitched at the scholars, it's for the deepest possible inner refreshment: drinking down one's worst calamities, laying them out in plain English, working your way through heartbreak, and arising fierce with hope and girded in steel. My kind of writing!

And here we are. We've stuck it out. Hey, I feel terrific, really awake. How did you like all this sun-dazzled Whitman, and Hemingway in Paris with his wine and oysters, and God tweaking Job with "Can you hold back the stars?" and John Edgar Wideman's massive tree of blackness with its trunk thick as a Buick, and Whitman singing the body electric, "the thin red jellies within you or within me," or Terry McMillan's Mama's headachy cupboard heavy-laden with beans and J. D. Salinger's Bessie Glass fingering through her crammed medicine chest, or my own wading through brown shit in the Erie sewer drains, or Thomas Wolfe's gargantuan midnight snack— "should it be the smoky pungency, the half-nostalgic savor of the Austrian ham" or a meal with the circus people wandering through the foods of America with their "big steaks for breakfast, hot from the pan and caked with onions," and "huge roasting ears of corn, smacking hot, piled like cord-wood on two-foot platters," or Wolfe's "face of the night, the heart of the dark, the tongue of the flame" as bleak men go "prowling up and down the empty pavements of bleak streets," or Whitman wandering all night in his vision of sleepers and his "I am he that walks with the tender and growing night—Press close bare-bosom'd night—Smile, for your lover comes," or Elizabeth Bowen's full moon drenching every niche of her bombed city—"London looked like the moon's capital—shallow, cratered, extinct," or Henry Beston's rainblack night of grassy waves falling on Nauset Beach, and Mailer's waves booming below a Provincetown window, or Ishmael's surly blackness in New Bedford—"Such dreary streets! blocks of blackness, not houses," or my wife Nancy's phosphorescent star-flower blooming in a black sea and her Armenian father's "apricot moon as big as a table top, Mary," or Louis L'Amour's Sackett walking his horse past "a few squat bristle-cone pines, gnarled from their endless war with the wind," or Raymond Chandler's Philip Marlowe—"What did it matter where you lay once you were dead? . . . You just slept the big sleep, not caring about the nastiness of how you died or where you fell"—or Conrad's Marlow going up the Congo mostly by inspiration, "its mysterious stillness watching me at my monkey tricks," or Robert Stone's Boschian nightmare on the soiled, starless New Jersey shore, or Father Egan's spiritual shock at the girl frozen in the beer cooler, or Nick Adams turning away from the tragic swamp in "Big Two-Hearted River," or Thoreau's dim, gloomy evening on the Merrimack River, or his gory battle of the ants at Walden, or George Amberson Minafer's befouled Indiana town and darkening sky and his comeuppance three times filled and running over, or Nick Carraway at Gatsby's party where the orchestra plays "yellow cocktail music," or the ghastly stomach-turning stinks and rankness of Patrick Suskind's eighteenth-century France and the perfumer's arts to cover them up, or Richard Selzer's tour of the human organs, their secret colors of maroon and salmon and yellow, or Hans Castorp's falling in love with Madame Chauchat's subcutaneous fat and his X ray of the bony framework of her ribs, "all shrouded in a dim and vaporous envelope of flesh," or Aschenbach's hopeless mortification under the barber's fingers in Venice, or Joan Didion's wipeout under the sultry Los Angeles Santa Ana, or "the peril, unspeakable peril, in the everyday" of her bungalows between Melrose and Sunset, or Carol Matthau's hard times gardening, wringing her hands at her pelvis in a cry of the heart against laughing selfish sonofabitch Walter, or her moving words about Oona on the death of Charlie Chaplin and Oona/Lucy Gayheart holding her bare arms out into the falling snow, or Capote's soufflé of bursting egg yolks and DRINK ME bottle of Roederer's Cristal at La Côte Basque, or Proust's clinical depression lifting as he trips on the curb going into the Guermantes' party, or Madame de Sévigné's thousand and one agonies about death in her letter to her daughter, or Charlotte Mew's large dead rat in the mud of the drive, and my telling her, "But, Charlotte, being buried isn't something you can hurry into," or Whitman's ruined whore unclaimed on the damp brick pavement at the Philadelphia morgue, dead, dead, dead, or Val's aria to Lady about the bird that sleeps on the wind and weighs no more than a feather but its wings spread this wide and are the color of the sky, or Edith Wharton's Newland Archer sighing in his opera box about his fiancée May's abysmal purity, or Norman Maclean's crown fires and fire whirls and the foreman lying down in embers to save himself, or Anaïs Nin's cutting the throat of the child diarist she once was, or Wild Bill's big aria about Cleopatra, cribbed from Plutarch, whose grandfather saw eight wild boars roasting at once in Cleo's kitchen, or Hemingway among the garbage scows on the Gulf Stream, or old Santiago rowing out into phosphorescent Gulf weed and later setting his big sweet-smelling, good-tasting baits at forty fathoms, or Mailer's Menenhetet having herbs and spices pounded into his cavity during the turquoise twilight of Egyptian evenings, or the Great God Tolstoy boring into Strider's mind and having his throat cut, or becoming the decomposing maggotty body of Serpukhovskoy, or Nadezhda Mandelstam's hope against hope for her imprisoned husband and horror that there might be nobody who could ever properly bear witness to the past, and dead Osip goes on memorizing new lines in the back rooms of his eyes, or my Drunkspearean catalog of alcoholic symptoms which I denied, or John Bunyan's Christian running off from his family with his fingers in his ears while the neighbors mocked, or Bunyan's imprisonment and "the pulling of flesh from bones" as he parts from his blind child? How did you like this Ninth Symphony of writers breathing together and lifting us all on their mighty sounds? Waking the dead! How did you like it?

Index